Benjamin Morgan Palmer

The Broken Home

Lessons in Sorrow

Benjamin Morgan Palmer

The Broken Home
Lessons in Sorrow

ISBN/EAN: 9783337778729

Printed in Europe, USA, Canada, Australia, Japan

Cover: Foto ©Thomas Meinert / pixelio.de

More available books at **www.hansebooks.com**

THE BROKEN HOME;

—OR—

Lessons in Sorrow,

—BY—

B. M. PALMER, Pastor,

FIRST PRESBYTERIAN CHURCH,

NEW ORLEANS, LA.

———

SECOND EDITION—1891.

———

E. S. UPTON,
Religious Book Depository,
NEW ORLEANS, LA.

INTRODUCTORY NOTE.

The following pages are committed to the Press, after no little mental conflict. The " stricken deer," says Cowper, withdraws

" To seek a tranquil death in distant shades :"

and so the mourner should hide his wound beneath his mantle. But the Free-Masonry of those in sorrow would pour the balm into other hearts which the Spirit of Consolation may have given to each.

From the simple desire of comforting those who mourn, this story of repeated bereavements is here told. It is proper to add, that the conversations reported in these sketches are copied verbatim from notes taken at the time. They are recited without enlargement or embellishment, that they may be the more touching from their simplicity. Long-treasured memories are now scattered upon the winds, with the prayer that they may help to " bind up the broken-hearted." THE AUTHOR.

"Oh, haunted soul,
Down whose dim corridors forever roll
The voices of the dead; whose holy ground
Re-echoes, at the midnight hour, with sound
Of feet that long ago were laid to rest,
Yet trouble thee forever! Lo, a guest
Is waiting at the gate; and unto Him
Thou shalt bemoan thy Dead, and He will take
Sweet words and comfort thee. Thine eyes are dim,
But stretch thine hands to Him; He will not break
The bruised reed."

I.

"A little fondling thing, that to my breast
   Clung always, either in quiet or unrest."

The morning was opening its eye in the first gray streak upon the horizon, when a faint cry issued from an upper chamber in one of our Southern cities. Instantly the hurried steps were arrested, of one pacing uneasily to and fro in the hall beneath. It was a cry which, when once heard, is never forgotten; the low, flat wail of a babe just entering a world to which it is a stranger— the symbol of pain, premonitory of all it must suffer between the cradle and the grave. It fell now, for the first time, upon ears which had ached through the weary night to catch the sound. The long suspense was over; and the deep sympathy which had taken up into the soul the anguish that another felt in the body, gave place to exultation when the great peril was passed. The young father bowed himself on the spot where he stood, and poured out an over-charged heart in grateful praise to Him who had softened the curse to " woman, who, being deceived, was in the transgression," by the gracious " notwithstanding she shall be saved in child-bearing, if they continue in faith and charity and holiness with sobriety."

Solemn thoughts crowd together in the first parental consciousness: thoughts that deepen in significance afterward; but never so startling as when they rush upon the soul in the first experience of the new relation. Shall they be embalmed in speech? Thousands in the rehearsal will recall the earliest flush of those emotions.

" Little miniature of myself—bone and flesh of my own substance—to whom I stand, as the instrumental cause of thy being, a secondary creator! Claiming by equal right the ancestral name, and wresting it from me when I am low in death! Soon to be strong and tall as I—coming each day more into the foreground, and pushing me nearer to the edge over which I must topple at the last! Sole occupant then of all my trusts; the mysterious link that binds me to the generations that follow, in whom all my earthly immortality resides; and passing me on but as a figure in the continuous succession! And yet, in all this formidable rivalry, I clasp this first-born to my heart with not the least infusion of jealousy.

"Little stranger, comest thou to solve or to darken the mystery of marriage? Even at the fountain, the stream was parted in two heads in the dualism of sex. Great enigma of Nature, lying just at the beginning: man's unity broken by the separateness of woman—yet preserved in her derivation from his side, ideally existing still in him from whom she was taken. The complementary parts are reintegrated into the whole by a mystical union which blends the two spiritually into one. And now the joint life issues in a birth: the child gathers into itself the double being from which it sprung, and diversity returns to the

unity whence it emerged. Strange recon-
ciliation of Nature's contradictions—this
third, in whom the one and the two are
brought together again. Tiny infant as
thou art, thou dost yet interpret the symbol of marriage to those who produced
thee.

"An immortal soul, with dormant
powers that by and by will compass the
universe; now soaring to the cope-stone
of heaven, and measuring the stars; now
turning the stone-leaves which beneath the
earth record the histories of countless
cycles. A soul which will at last strip off
the encumbrance of clay, and sweep with
exploring wing the vast eternity where
God makes His dwelling place. And I
must stoop beneath this wing and teach its
first flight, that will rise higher and higher
in the far forever.

"A soul, alas, born under the curse of
sin, through me the guilty channel. And
I must stand in the holy priesthood ap-
point d of God, between it and eternal
death. My soul must be in its soul's stead,

and feel for it the Law's penal frown. My
faith must lay her hand upon the covenant,
' I will be a God to thee and to thy seed
after thee ; ' and plead the force of that
great instrument with all the agony of
human intercession."

Such were the thoughts that, like rolling
waves, flooded the heart of the young pastor ; who found in these new responsibilities
a divinity school, with richer teachings
than that which had trained and sent him
forth to his lifework. A grand theology
was forming itself out of these experiences ;
where every thought was turned into
prayer, and knowledge glided into worship. With muffled tread he ascended the
stairway ; and stood beside one who in the
shaded light was pale as the sheet on which
she lay. A new word was born upon his
lips, which softly whispered, " Mother,
we are three."

Two and twenty months rolled away,
and the boy grew. Ah! there are proud
moments in every man's domestic life. It
is an epoch when before the altar he feels

the trust trembling upon his arm, of the gentle being who dares with him to face life's great uncertainty—a trust the stronger, because it trembles. In rude boyhood I once snared a dove. But when it turned its soft eyes upward, and I felt upon my palm the throb of its frightened heart, I relented and cast it forth to the freedom of its own wing again. It was God's way of teaching gentleness, even through a bird ; and the lesson went down into the character which it helped to mould. But this confiding heart, which beat against my own in that hour of vows, fluttered with no pulse of fear; only with an awe over-shadowing the supreme moment in which the after years are wedged, and their dark contingencies ; and it was the pride of honest manhood that fixed the resolve, to conquer life for her and to make its very harshness smooth.

So, too, with a proud joy the father tosses his first-born into the air, and re-ceives him back screaming with delight, in utter unconsciousness of any peril. This

strange commingling of robust mirth with
childhood's rollicking gaiety, are they not
threads woven into the family life every-
where? And then the more thoughtful
pride with which a father bends over the
sleeping babe and casts its horoscope.
Life, short though it be, is it not filled with
mere repetitions? We scarcely begin to
realize the prophecies of our own youth,
before we drop into the lives of our children in dreamy anticipations of their future.

Thus during these twenty months pious
hopes were springing up in this young
father's musing. Through generations co-
eval with the history of the country, as far
back as the lineage could be traced, the
prophet's mantle had rested upon an honor-
able ancestry. From sire to son the oil of
consecration had been poured on those who,
as ambassadors of Christ, had besought
men to be reconciled unto God. Would
the blessed succession be continued in the
generations to come? At the entrance of
his own calling, he looked through the
vista of years to the goal when he must lay

it down; and with the fervor of his own consecration, he prayed that the family traditions might be preserved in this scion of a priestly line.

Ah, ye who pray, know ye the mode in which the answer is returned? "We walk by faith, not by sight;" and it needs a purged eye to read the faithfulness of God in our bitter disappointments. Whilst in visions of the future the young minister was casting his robe of office upon the child of his loins, an angel's wing touched the babe and dropped into its cradle the call to higher ministries beyond the stars. It was seen in the earthly blight which shrivelled up the little form, until the loose flesh lapped over the thin bones like an unfitting garment. The hunger of disease could find nothing for its insatiate voracity, but the juices of the body on which it fed ; and the breathing skeleton lay at length upon a pillow on the mother's lap. How old the child grew in two short months, and how tall its little limbs became ! Every trace of infantile beauty was effaced, only

the golden curls floated over the pale.
brow; and the brilliant eyes which strangers
in the street stooped to gaze upon, burned
now with a feverish lustre. Half closed in
the uneasy sleep of sickness, even death
itself could not seal them up. In his very
coffin they peered out from beneath the
soft lashes with what looked so much like
thoughtfulness, that a creeping came over
the observer; wondering whether pain
could be a teacher, or if death could impress what seemed so like the reflection of
knowledge. It is more than forty years
since then, and the frost of winter has
whitened the hairs upon that father's head;
but across the stretch of all those years
two hazel eyes, bright as coals of Juniper,
still burn before his vision; and the memory is fresh as yesterday of that oldish look,
coming out of eternity and resting upon
that dying infant. Ah! who can tell how
the two worlds may overlap at the border
where they touch; or the way of "the
free Spirit" in His dealing with a soul
standing at the gates of Heaven? The

great mystery of death, how it swallows up
the lesser mysteries of life which are so
perplexing! Reader, in that narrow hour
we shall touch them all; and the great
revelation will come next after, in the light
of the Throne.

Hope and fear kept the scales evenly in
the balance, for a time; but at length the
beam went down, and fear deepened into
anguish. As the grim certainty became
each day more sure, there was another
pacing to and fro in the little room where
the oil was beaten for the sanctuary; and
solemn questions came up from beneath
the Judgment seat, and shook the heart of
him who felt that he was sponsor for his
child.

"This little soul which I had hoped to
lead through knowledge up to God, must
I not lead it still in another way, seeing
that He calls for it from above? Ah,
Saviour, if this be Thy voice saying as of
old, "of such is the kingdom of Heaven,"
who am I that I should ·forbid? If to be
taken into Thine arms is to be blessed

forever, then, like the Hebrew mothers,
let me bring this little one to Thee,
even in death, for the great benediction.
Oh, troubled heart, be still, and learn
that no selfishness can be in love;
that He who loves his Master with-
holds nothing, when He has need of it;
and he who loves his child will sink all
sense of loss in the everlasting gain to it,
of lying safe upon the bosom of the Shep-
herd." Thus the sharp struggle between
nature and grace was ended in the submission which said, "not my will, but thine,
be done." It was the first lesson that came
out of the first sorrow.

Was this submission hard to learn? Yet
it was implicitly contained in the full surrender of the soul to God in penitence and
faith, long before made. It was only the
bringing out, in special form, what had in
principle been wrought within by the Spirit
of God. The life of the seed can only pass
into the life of the plant, under the patient
discipline of nature; and so the principial
virtue implanted in the new birth passes,

only under the discipline of grace, into the active experience of the believer. But if this lesson was taught the father and the Christian, there was another which entered into the lifework of the pastor and teacher.

This child, could it suffer thus except under the law of sin? Could death seize upon it, except it lay beneath the curse? No article of faith was more firmly held by him than this, "By one man sin entered into the world, and death by sin; and so death passed upon all men, for that all have sinned;" and this, "Death reigned from Adam to Moses, even over them that had not sinned after the similitude of Adam's transgression, which is the figure of Him that was to come." It was, however, no cold abstraction lying in the black-letter of a creed, but a living and fearful responsibility which now rolled itself upon the conscience.

Thus he soliloquized: "This suffering infant is through me the heir of human guilt, and derives from me a nature stained with the defilement of sin. How, then,

shall it appear before the God of dreadful
holiness? If through me it sustains this
relation to the law and the curse, does it
sustain through me no relation to the grace
which shall work its deliverance from both?
If bound through me a sinner in firm connection with the first Adam, by whom is
'the judgment to condemnation'—do I not
stand, as a believer, a link between it and
the second Adam, by whom is 'the free
gift unto justification?' Think, my soul,
of the solemn sponsorship which roots
itself in the parental relation. What did
it mean, when I gave this child to God in
the covenant of baptism? When, on its
behalf, I confessed the sinful estate in which
it was born, and its need of redemption by
the blood of Christ? What did Jehovah
mean when He responded in the gracious
promise, 'I will be a God to thy seed after
thee?' What did it mean when, with the
water of consecration upon its brow, the
Lord placed the infant in my arms and
said, 'Nurse it for me and I will give thee
thy wages?' And when in the public

assembly I vowed to train it in the nurture
and admonition of the Lord, as belonging
to Him and to Him alone? Was this an
idle ceremony of the Church, only the
dramatic form in which she chose to cast
her teaching? Or was it rather a true
covenant which the great and mighty God
made with me and with my house ; that in
like manner as by the law of nature the
curse descended through me upon my offspring, so by the law of grace the blessing
should entail, through the operation of my
faith, upon the children of my loins?"

In the opening of a minstry which God
designed to be long upon earth, this death
of his first-born let the young Pastor down
into the mysteries of that covenant which
he should afterward expound. But not
yet did it crystallize in any form of doctrine. It lay upon his heart only as a tre-
mendous fact, that, in all these solemn
transactions of grace, he stood for his child ;
and that his faith must lay hold upon the
covenant in its behalf, and plead for its
salvation in some sort as he once pleaded

for his own. Under these convictions it did
not suffice coolly to assume that infants,
dying before they can discern between
good and evil, are saved from death eternal by the simple necessity of the case.
This might be so ; or, better still, the early
removal of such before the possibility of
actual transgression may be the pledge of
their election through grace, and the precise condition upon which their salvation
must turn. These traditional beliefs had
long been cherished by him before whom
deeper views were now opening, and had
wrought themselves as firm convictions in
his soul. But something more than bare
opinion was needed to sustain one who
stood confronted by a double sponsorship
under the law of nature and of grace. By
the one, he became the channel through
which a corrupt nature was transmitted ;
by the other, he was solemnly constituted
the representative of his offspring in the
eternal covenant which pledged eternal
life to the faith which would accept its
provisions. The one transaction was as

real as the other; and while the spiritual
life was not conveyed through carnal
descent like the spiritual death, yet the
law of grace, which evermore demands
faith of its recipient, seems to require its
vicarious exercise for such as in the covenant were dealt with by and through a
sponsor.   To this father, at least, the bap-
tismal vow meant that, if it meant anything
at all.   It became him now to put his soul
in the stead of his first-born.   He must feel
the shame of that dishonor which sin had
cast upon it.   He must take upon his conscience the burden of its guilt, to confess
and bewail it before God.   Having learned
for himself to rest upon the atonement of
Christ for pardon and eternal life, he must
now exercise this faith for the child, which
the child cannot exercise for itself.   He
must plead in its behalf the Divine promise
which, under the constitution of grace, he
had been appointed a sponsor to plead.
Unspeakably solemn was the trust, when
the reality of it came to be understood and
felt.   More than the life of a generation

has passed, since he thus bowed himself
before God with an agony of wrestling
scarcely less than that with which he prayed
in the hour of his first conviction as a sinner; but all eternity will never efface the
impression then made upon his spirit, nor
undo the influence which it exerted upon
his whole Christian experience afterward.
Days were spent in wrestling intercession—
days which were darkened with awe under
a sense of this fearful trust; until at length
a peace broke upon the soul, like the peace
which first lifted the burden of sin in his
own conversion.   A blessed token was enjoyed that his prayers had gone up as a
memorial before God; and he sat beside
his dying boy with the strong comfort of
believing that the promise of the covenant
was assured to his seed forever.   Other
children were born later, who lived to grow
up and confess Christ for themselves before
the world.   But never from this moment
did a shade of doubt cloud his faith—that
He who had gathered so early the first-
fruits of his household into His garner,

would gather the increase when that, too, should be ripe.   And this was the second lesson, solemn yet gracious, which came out of the first sorrow ; teaching what it was to be a Christian father, standing before God the representative of his offspring.

Nineteen years bright with happiness and love had chased far away the gloom of that bereavement.   Even the memory of it grew faint, as it shaded off in the distance ; or when recalled, was recalled without a pang for the richness of the blessing that lay in it and had sanctified the years which came after.   It was destined to be brought near again, by a relic which the grave itself should yield.   Nineteen years of sunshine, and then the voice of weeping was heard again.   Another grave must be dug, to receive the second-born.   She was laid to rest in a beautiful cemetery, upon the bank of a stream whose gentle flow murmured a soft and constant dirge over the sleepers by its side.   It was a new City of the Dead, which taste and art sought to adorn : vain tribute of love to those who heed it

not. "Let the two lie together," said the
parents as they wept : and we will carve
upon the marble of the one,

"The little angel smiled and slept;"

and upon the marble of the other,

"She who, gentle as a saint,
Ne'er gave us pain."

And so the pick-axe and the shovel threw
aside the earth which for many years had
pressed upon the bosom of the infant.
Only a few bones and the little skull. No,
wait a second; and with trembling hand
the father clipped one little curl from which
the lustre had faded, but twining still
around the hollow temple. He placed it
on the palm of his hand, without a word,
before the eye of the mother. With a
smothered cry she fell upon his neck—
"It is our boy's ; I see it as long ago, the
soft lock that curled upon his temple."
"Take it, mother; it is to us the prophecy
of the Resurrection ; the grave has not the
power to destroy." The old tears were
wept again ; but through them God made
the rainbow to shine.

The following lines, which may be found in the Biography of Mr. Webster, are not generally known.   Beneath the rugged versification lurks a genuine pathos; showing the great statesman not to have been destitute of the sentiment which marks the Poet:

"My Son! thou wast my heart's delight,
  Thy morn of life was gay and cheery;
That morn has rushed to sudden night,
  Thy father's house is sad and dreary.

" I held thee on my knee, my Son,
  And kissed thee laughing, kissed thee weeping;
But ah, thy little day is done,
  Thou'rt with thy angel sister sleeping.

"The staff on which my years should lean
  Is broken, ere those years come o'er me;
My funeral rites thou shouldst have seen,
  But thou art in the grave before me.

"Thou rear'st to me no filial stone,
  No parent's grave with tears beholdest;
Thou art my Ancestor, my Son,
  And stand'st in Heaven's account the oldest.

"On earth my lot was soonest cast,
  Thy generation after mine;
Thou hast thy predecessor past—
  Earlier Eternity is thine.

" I should have set before thine eyes
   The road to Heaven, and showed it clear ;
   But thou untaught spring'st to the skies,
   And leav'st thy teacher lingering here.

" Sweet Seraph, I would learn of thee,
   And hasten to partake thy bliss ;
   And oh, to thy world welcome me,
   As first I welcomed thee to this.

" Dear Angel, thou art safe in Heaven ;
   No prayers for thee need more be made ;
   Oh, let thy prayers for those be given
   Who oft have blessed thy infant head.

" My Father, I beheld thee born,
   And led thy tottering steps with care ;
   Before me risen to Heaven's bright morn,
   My Son, my Father, guide me there."

II.

"But lying darkly between,
  Winding down through the night,
  Is the dim and unknown stream
  That leads at last to the light."

Months elapsed before the voice of childhood broke the oppressive stillness. A daughter was then clasped to the mother's breast, who said: "This now shall comfort us for our first-born, whom the Lord has taken." The cloud had drifted away which threw the first shadow upon us, and the sky was bright with the smile of God for nineteen years. The little comforter who crept first into our hearts, in due time gave her sisterly welcome to others who came after; until a group of five daughters chased away the gloom of the early death, and the house rang again with gladness and song. Almost the half of wedded life was spent without a tear to moisten the eye, or a

pang to pierce the heart. The infinitely
wise Father above will educate us for
Heaven and Himself through joy as well
as sorrow. Under the double influence of
the sunshine and the rain the fruitful earth
will yield her increase to the husbandman.

But the smile and the tear, do they simply succeed each other? Or is the one
the fountain from which the other flows?
Is there a joy on earth, which does not
hide in its bosom the kindred grief that
shall presently flood the soul? Within the
bloom, lies the blight of every flower—
within the life, lies hid the death of all who
make us happy. As, on the other hand,

> "The night is mother of the day,
> And winter of the spring ;
> And ever upon old decay
> The greenest mosses spring."

The baby girl that dropped upon us in our
sadness, brought a blessing with her from
the skies ; and left a blessing, when she
went up again to weave a new tie for us
above. Her infancy was bright and full of
cheer, with those little endearments which
make a babe a sunbeam in the home. The

development of mind came on apace, with
the usual pride in those precocious utterances, which to fond parents are the proofs
of infantile genius. As education ad-
vanced, she disclosed a quick understanding which gathered knowledge with ease;
so that under a generous culture of eighteen years she was fitted to adorn any
station in life. Her virtues were of the
quiet kind: gentle and unobtrusive in **her**
bearing she won the affection of all, while
her singleness and sincerity of character
secured their confidence and trust. She
was singularly free from all censoriousness
of spirit: never indulging in the sharpness
of personal criticism herself, it was thor-
oughly distasteful to her in others. She
was ever ready to palliate the faults which
drew forth the language of censure, setting
over against these the virtues of those who
were the subjects of animadversion. At
an early age she united with the Church of
God, and through her brief life "adorned
the doctrine of God her Saviour in all
things." She was one whose "faults

leaned to virtue's side:" and the single
weakness of her character must be empha-
sized in order to explain what will follow
in this sketch of her dying hours. Her
diffidence and humility deepened into
timidity and self-distrust which, even in
her school-life, marred her happiness. She
was never satisfied with her preparations
for the class-room, often prolonging her
studies to extreme weariness of body and
mind.   Like the steed whose mettle fails
only with expiring life, I have sometimes
feared that this continued friction wore
upon her delicate and susceptible nature ;
and that the strain of so much anxiety and
toil may have sapped the strength which
was needed to resist the insidious disease
that so soon attacked her frame.   It will
be instructive at least to notice how natural
temperament often modifies our Christian
experience, giving a shape and color it
would not otherwise present.   This outline
of her recognized traits will introduce to
the reader the record of her illness and
death.

In the month of May, 1862, we first noticed a slight cough, which we attributed, as usual, to a cold; and hoped it would wear off. It increased, however, instead of diminishing, and was accompanied with expectoration. She began to pine away, and complained of lassitude. The civil war which then convulsed the country, had thrown us from our home; but as soon as we had found permanent quarters as refugees, her lungs were sounded by a skilful physician, who could detect only a little dullness at the base of the right lung. She continued to decline throughout the winter, but was able to go about and ride on horseback; a kind of exercise which we encouraged as peculiarly beneficial. Towards spring her appetite, always delicate, became capricious; and she began to look emaciated.

Early in April, 1863, her mother took her to the seaboard, hoping that a visit to relatives, with change of scene and diet, would rally her failing powers and rouse her drooping spirits. Instead of this she

declined so rapidly that we feared she
might not be able to return. In May, I
went for her, and was comforted by the
apparent ease with which she accomplished
the journey back. But her appetite was
completely gone ; she loathed food more
than physic. No delicacies tempted her
palate ; and she hung for weeks at this
point, wasted to a skeleton—getting no
better, and apparently no worse.

A certain service was laid upon me by
the Church which required my presence in
the Army of Tennessee, and I was in great
mental conflict as to my personal duty.
Though I had resigned all hope of her recovery, it seemed probable that she would
linger many months ; accordingly I resolved
to leave her with her mother and with God.
But how shall I describe the agony of that
parting ? She wept convulsively ; that
poor wasted frame shook with sobs upon
that dying bed ; and my heart was almost
as much broken as her own. She uttered
only one cry : "Father, you are going so
far, and I am so ill." Oh ! how the words

kept ringing in my ears amidst the drums and cannon of the camp; and I could not but ask myself daily, if duty did indeed require me to be thus cruel to my dying child. She evidently feared it was a final separation; which, thanks to God, it did not prove to be. I took advantage of the confusion of the retreat from Shelbyville, to run home and look upon the pale face once more. It was early morning when I arrived, and she was still asleep. Awaking in a few moments, she burst into tears and exclaimed twice: "I knew he would come; I knew he would come!" Just as a ray of light illumines a dark room, so this one sentence revealed to me the thoughts that had been passing through her mind. It was a word so full of love, so full of trust, that I bowed over her and wept like a woman. There was another cause for tears: my eyes, not beguiled as were the eyes of others by the gradual progress of the disease, detected at once the signature of the tomb upon that smooth white brow; and I resolved instantly never to leave her until

she was yielded in the Saviour's arms.
This was on the fourth of July; and for
eleven days no presage of immediate death
was afforded. During the night of the
fifteenth violent pains, which had been re-
pressed by astringent remedies, returned
with all their former intensity ; but yielded
to external applications, and ceased altogether about the hour of breakfast next
morning. It was the beginning of the end,
but we knew it not. During the forenoon
one slight cough brought up a mouthful of
phlegm, and was followed by fainting arrested only upon the border of unconsciousness. This occurred three times
during the day. I thought the fainting
only nervous ; the mother, with the truer
instinct of her sex, saw in it dissolution.
So it proved ; for at half-past ten that night
she was in Heaven.

Throughout her sickness I had been
averse to speaking with her on the subject
of death : partly from the confidence I felt
in her preparation for the great change—
partly from unwillingness to extinguish the

last spark of hope which, in one so feeble,
I feared might extinguish the last spark of
life—but mainly from an unmanly weakness that sought to hide from sight a truth
so unwelcome. So much are we like the
ruined bankrupt, who has not the courage
to look his insolvency fairly in the face.
I have since deeply regretted this reticence;
since longer and more frequent conversations might have contributed towards removing the painful apprehensions which I
afterwards found to burden her mind.

On Sabbath afternoon, July 12th, under
a simple sense of duty, I first broke through
this reserve. Lying upon the bed by her
side, the following conversation took place:

"My daughter, I would like to know
what you think of your case; do you
think you will ever recover?"

"No, father, I do not see how it is possible for me to get well."

"Do you feel then, F——, that you are
prepared to die?"

"Yes, father, I hope I am ready; but I
feel so very unworthy."

"What is it, daughter, that makes you feel so unworthy ?"

"Oh, I have lived so far below my duty."

Supposing that she referred to neglect of her accustomed devotions since her extreme sickness, of which she had spoken once before, I said :

"You are too weak now to attend to these in form ; it is enough for you to lift up your heart to God upon your bed."

"I do not mean that," she replied ; "I know that God cares nothing for posture : I refer to my whole Christian life since I joined the Church ; I often fear that I made a profession of religion prematurely : when I was at school I was obliged to sit up late at night, and was so sleepy that my prayers were frequently a mere form."

I reminded her of Christ's apology for His disciples, when they slept through weakness in the Garden ; and said to her :

"Jesus is no hard taskmaster—could He not make allowance for your infirmity, as well as for that of Peter, James and John ?"

"Yes, father, I sometimes think of that: but I look back on my whole Christian life, and it is worth just nothing. I have often feared that I may be deceived."

"Those," I replied, "who dread being deceived seldom are so; because it lies in the nature of the delusion that it is not even suspected. But, F——, there is a short cut out of this difficulty; for we are saved after all, not by our goodness, but by Christ Jesus, in whom we believe."

"Oh, yes, I know that; and there is all my hope."

"Do you feel then, my daughter, that you place your whole trust in the Saviour of sinners?"

"Yes, I feel that my trust is in Christ alone."

"Well, then, you are not afraid to die?"

"No, not exactly; but, father, it is a fearful thing to die."

"So it is, my darling, to the impenitent; but to God's children it is but going home."

"Yes, if we could only have but perfect assurance that we are His children."

The above conversation was held just five days before her death, and when there was no symptom of its near approach. She was apparently in the same condition as during months previous. The next clear intimation of her hope in Christ was given in her first fainting spell, on the day of her death. Construing it as the approach of the last enemy, she exclaimed :

"Oh, mother, I am dying!"

Her mother replied, with much agitation :

"Daughter, I believe you are; trust your Saviour."

Unable to speak at the moment, her mouth being filled with phlegm she had just coughed up, she assented with a cheerful energetic nod of the head, so familiar to those who knew her well, which she frequently employed to indicate a hearty and emphatic assent; and as soon as she could speak, added with great promptness and earnestness, "I do, I do," and then sank back exhausted.

In the afternoon of the same day, after her third fainting spell, I was seated on the bed by her, when she turned and said:

"Father, it is a frightful thing to die."

I answered:

"My daughter, you have twice said that to me: what is there in death that seems to you so fearful?"

"Oh, it is such a solemn thing to meet God. But what I most dread is the pain of dying."

It was a great relief to learn that the cause of apprehension was only this; and I answered:

"You may dismiss, my darling, all alarm on that score: I am well convinced, from seeing many persons die, that in the moment of death there is no consciousness of pain."

I have since learned that the special thought which haunted her was the fear of strangling, from inability at the last to expectorate. I continued:

"F——, do you feel that you love Jesus?"

She answered promptly :

"Yes, I know that I love Him."

"Do you know that you love Him, just as you know that you love your mother and me ?"

"Just in the same way," she replied.

"Well, then, if you love Him and He loves you, can you not leave this matter of your dying in His hands, without being distressed; just, for example, as you have often left things to your mother and me, and have given yourself no further concern, simply because you confided both in our wisdom and affection?"

She answered, "Yes." As she was very feeble, I did not press the conversation further ; especially as I did not even then suspect her end to be so near.

After tea I came into the room and fixed her more comfortably upon the bed and pillow. It was the last time any one was called to dispose her poor emaciated form ; and she lay in that position to the end.

Presently she said :

"Mother, turn on the gas and give more light."

I walked to the mantel and found a full jet of flame already burning, and said:

"It cannot be any brighter, my daughter; does it not seem bright to you?"

"No, it appears to be getting dark," she replied.

One of the avenues of this world of sense was closing its portal to her; and this first discovered to us that she was actually dying. I was startled, too, by the fact that her voice, hitherto so weak as to compel us to bend our ears to her lips, had become strong; and was heard with a ringing sound over the room. It was another harbinger of death. Her mother and I drew close to her side, where one of her sisters was faithfully fanning her. She looked round and asked for another sister, who was hidden behind her mother; whom she immediately addressed:

"Pray for me, M——, that I may pass gently away."

She then called for the two remaining

sisters; and seeing them both sobbing, said:

"You must not cry for me, when I am gone; for you know that I am obliged to go."

She then called for her grandmother, who was preparing some nourishment for her during the night. As she delayed a little, F—— became impatient. A second message was sent to her, to leave everything and come at once. Upon entering the room she was startled at seeing us all weeping around the bed. She asked:

"What is it you want of me, my daughter?"

"Nothing, grandmother, only to see you once more; as I am going very fast."

"Is Jesus very precious to you?" asked the grandmother.

"Oh, yes, He is very precious," was the sweet reply.

One was bathing her hand with cologne: she exclaimed, "How delightful!" Turning to a servant who was bathing the other hand across the bed, and alluding to the recent death of an old family servant, said :

"Maum Lucy did not go much before me."

Her mother asked if she did not wish to see a relative whom she named. She replied :

"Yes, I have not seen him for several days."

As he entered and came to her bedside, she said :

"G——, take warning; but you have been warned before"— alluding to a brother's death about a year before.

She was asked if she desired to send a message to a kinswoman recently married, and now absent :

"Yes, tell her I wish she was here ; she little dreams of this ; she is happy now—I hope we will soon meet again."

Other messages were sent to absent cousins, to whom she had always been attached :

"Give R—— my love, and tell him—he knows what I would say to him."

Thinking she was growing weary, I inquired:

"F——, are you not tired talking?"

"Yes, but you know I did not commence to talk soon;" and added:

"I wish I could have seen the doctor again; give him my love."

It was asked:

"Would you like your grandfather to pray for you?"

"Yes;" but as he was about to begin she interposed:

"I want to say one thing more: Mother, when you get back to our old home, give my love to every one who cares for me, and to the servants, too."

Turning then to her grandfather, and placing her hand in his, she said:

"You may pray now, grandfather; and pray that I may pass gently away."

He offered a very touching prayer on her behalf; after which she turned to me and said:

"Father, I hope I shall not be disappointed; no, not disappointed—you know what I mean; you know I was always a timid child."

"I think, daughter, I know what you mean: there is no danger of your being disappointed; the Saviour will fulfil all His promises to you."

Looking tenderly upon us, she said:

"I hope we shall all soon meet again."

After a little, raising her arms with an emphatic gesture, she cried:

"Mother, I declare I am getting right deaf!"

Another avenue was closing, of the poor world she was rapidly leaving. From this time she was silent, except that upon her groaning twice her mother asked:

"What is the matter, F——, does any place hurt you?"

"Nothing, mother; only sinking, sinking, sinking away"—accompanying the utterance with a gradual lowering of the hand three times in the air. She then became somewhat delirious, holding imaginary conversations with absent persons. In this delirium she appeared distressed, and whined aloud as a child about to cry. I called aloud to her, making myself heard with difficulty by the dull cold ear of death:

"F——, my daughter, what troubles you?"

Rousing to consciousness, she turned her eyes upon me, and said simply:

"Father, Father;" but with an inflection of tone I cannot indicate on paper, and which I can never forget—so full of love and trust, as though she would still lean upon me while going down into the Dark Valley. It was the last sound from her blessed lips. She sank into silence—a silence only to be broken as her clear silvery voice rang out amidst the praises of the Upper Temple. Her respiration became quicker, her pulse more thread-like—one short spasm passed over her frame—she gently raised her elbow as though she would fly, and the tragic scene was closed! The poor wasted body was with us; the rejoicing spirit was with the harpers, veiling itself before the glories of the Throne.

The story is almost told. One day and night we watched by the dust so precious in our eyes; and on the 19th of July, 1863, we laid her down by the side of her infant brother, to sleep until the trumpet's call. But the agony of turning away and leaving her alone—leaving her alone whom we had so tenderly cherished, that no wind of heaven blew roughly upon her, this, O God! is known only to Thee and to us. But we have exceeding comfort in this loss. We have no misgivings as to her eternal happiness. She had afforded while in life and health the most abundant evidence of a change of heart; and during her long illness, as she often said, "this world was dead to her." The apprehension of death which she expressed arose from constitutional timidity; which was sunk at last in a calm, clear trust in her Redeemer—except as she dreaded its physical pangs, which, thanks to God, she was mercifully spared.

Besides all this, she has left behind a most precious memory. I cannot say of her all that I could, lest I should be deemed extravagant; or, at least, lie open to the suspicion that, as death throws a halo over the departed, I am under the spell of a fond and delusive affection.   Yet I have said of her, long before this sad bereavement, since she was twelve years of age I could find nothing in her to amend.   Watching over her with a parent's anxiety to mould her character aright, there was nothing to correct.   She has left a memory in which there is nothing we would desire changed: as we travel over it in thought, every spot is green and lovely to the eye.   I had learned to reverence her.   The attributes which she displayed were so beautiful that I, who sought to shape and guide her aright, was often reproved by a virtue superior to my own.   Strange that we did not see through all those years that God was secretly educating her for Himself; and when she was ripe, she was plucked to be with Him. Her memory is a sweet and awful thing to us: we think of her not as dead, but as translated to be with Christ.   Our lovely flower bloomed awhile on its earthly stem, and then

"She was exhaled—her Creator drew
Her spirit, as the sun the morning dew."

The lesson taught in this second sorrow is the special grace reserved for a dying hour ; which will subdue the fears of the most timid and enable them to depart in peace, if not in triumph. Many reasons can be assigned for this dread of death, styled by the Apostle "the last enemy." There is the natural instinct of life, which we share with the beasts of the field ; a wholesome protection against the madness of despair which so often rushes its victim on to the guilt of suicide.   There is, again, the awfulness of death as the penalty of the broken Law.   How unnatural the separation of the soul and body, is shown when the spirit lingers in its tenement of clay and escapes reluctantly at last with the gurgling breath.   Is it possible, again, to shake off the ties of life from which the soul has through years been drawing the sweetness of earthly bliss, and not feel the pain ?   Add to these our ignorance as to the details of a Future State, disabling even the imagination from transporting us to its scenes and pursuits.   Finally, bring before the mind the pangs of dissolution, exaggerated often to the senses through the spasms of the body as it stretches to its death stature.   Aggregate all these terrors in one single conception, and the wonder will be, not that death is an object of dread, but that Christian hope should be strong enough to overcome it at the last. The history just recited is only one of many, going to show that with the most sensitive and shrinking of mortals this fear is quelled at the moment of passing into the presence of our King.   It is a grace reserved for this precise moment, guaranteed only then as the experience which is needed ; and is possibly connected with the last acts of the Holy Ghost in completing the believer's sanctification.   It has been said that the dying never weep ; certainly the composure is beyond the power

of nature, with which the dying saint yields
up all the companionships of life, and sun-
ders the dearest bonds of love. Ah, who
can tell what new joys swell the bosom of
the Christian the moment his feet touch
the stones of the Covenant, as he follows
the Ark "in the swelling of Jordan!"

The following lines depict the fierceness
of the conflict between fear and faith, in
many a timid Christian's breast:

"The way is dark, my Father! Cloud on cloud
Is gathering thickly o'er my head, and loud
The thunders roar above me. See, I stand
Like one bewildered! Father, take my hand,
  And through the gloom
  Lead safely home
   Thy child!

"The day goes fast, my Father! and the night
Is drawing darkly down. My faithless sight
Sees ghostly visions. Fears, a spectral band,
Encompass me. O Father! take my hand,
  And from the night
  Lead up to light
   Thy child!

" The throng is great, my Father!   Many a doubt
  And fear and danger compass me about;
  And foes oppress me sore.   I cannot stand
  Or go alone.   O Father! take my hand,
        And through the throng
        Lead safe along
          Thy child!

·" The cross is heavy, Father!   I have borne
  It long, and still do bear it.   Let my worn
  And fainting spirit rise to that blest land
  Where crowns are given.   Father! take my hand;
        And, reaching down,
        Lead to the crown
          Thy child!"

III.

"I hear a voice you cannot hear,
    Which says, I must not stay,
I see a hand you cannot see.
    Which beckons me away."

Our fourth daughter was from birth singularly attractive in appearance, possessing
features whose beauty time might improve,
but could never diminish.   Her eyes were
of a dark brown color, large and full of
lustre, yet liquid and soft.   In this feature,
as well as in a clear brunette complexion,
she resembled her only brother, the first-
born and the early taken of our little flock;
except that in his there was a pensiveness
of expression, as though it might be the
shadow of premature thought; and which
even after death still looked forth from the
half-closed lids, like a sort of revelation
from the upper world haunting the memory
through long years, and not wholly ban-

ished yet. Her hair deepening into the
darkest shade this side of black, and fine
as silk, curled in ringlets around her infant neck; growing afterwards into long
and graceful tresses that were gathered in
braids and folds around her head, after the
fashion of the time. In stature she was a
little above the medium height. Her only
defect was a narrowness of the chest—a
prognostic to the jealous love that watched
her growth of the fatal disease, which,
alas ! was soon to hurry her to the grave.
With gentle sloping shoulders and tapering
waist, her figure was complete in symmetry.
Over her person was diffused an air of
quiet dignity and ease, rendering her womanhood as full of grace as her infancy
was of beauty ; while in those dark eyes,
soft as those of a gazelle, lay the deep look
so full of soul—the pledge of affection
which would never deceive, and of character which would never betray. Alas,
that the beautiful should ever die ! But
God will be served with what we value
most; and we will not be envious of Him,

who has plucked from our garden the flower whose fragrance was so pleasing to us.

An incident of her infant life, which had almost faded from remembrance, looms up since her death with a weird and almost prophetic significance. When ten months old, it became necessary to break a slow fever by the use of quinine. Through a mistake wholly unaccountable, morphine was administered; the effect of which became soon too obvious. It was a hot day in July, on the Saturday preceding the communion Sabbath. Pulpit preparation and everything else were thrown aside as the little babe, pale and pulseless as though chiselled from Parian marble, lay upon the mother's knee in a state of coma. Five hours of ceaseless labor were spent by a skilful physician before the first sign of conscious life appeared; followed through six other distressing hours, by the fierce battle against the fatal slumber which, unresisted, must soon wrap the little form in the folds of that sleep which knows no waking It was a day of unspeakable an-

guish, remembered like some horrible
dream which once froze the heart with
terror. The mother rushed from chamber
to chamber in the frenzy of grief, at having
administered with her own loving hand the
dread potion: the father bowed the knee
in prayer and the vow that, if a merciful
God would but spare the child long enough
to break the connection with this tragical
accident, and so lift the self-accusing burden from the mother's heart, he would at
any moment resign the child to Him who
should grant so gracious a reprieve. The
prayer was heard, and after eighteen years
the moment came to redeem the vow.

" Be still, my soul, each groan suppress :
The child to thee in prayer twice given
Thy home with so much love to bless,
A solemn vow had pledged to Heaven.'

The sequel of this incident is as mysterious as the story is affecting. When the
child thus wonderfully spared grew old
enough to talk, her baby accents lisped
continually of another world. I will give
it in the childish words which, though long

since uttered, are graven on the memory as with the point of a diamond.

" When I went to Heaven," she used to say, " I saw a big white gate with a man standing just inside. Before it was a pool of water with a board across it ; and the man said, ' Come in, Sissy, but don't fall in.' But I fell in ; and he took me out into a room where there were a great many glory-children, and dressed me in white with wings like theirs. Then he took me to see God. I saw a big red pillow, with five black dots, that God rests on. And, mother, there were two gold rocking chairs for you and father, and five little ones for us children. And, Mauma (her nurse), there was a beautiful white satin dress for you ; it felt so smooth ; just put your hand on your hair, it felt just like that. I wanted to bring it to you ; but when I went to take it, it just slipped away. And now I spend every Sunday in Heaven, with God. He puts a ladder down for me every Saturday evening, and I go up and come home on Monday."

Strange words these, for a lisping babe of only three summers. Can Philosophy explain them? Was it but an infant's dream? But whence the ideas out of which its details were woven? She was too young to have gathered much out of St. John's Revelation, as that portion of God's word might happen to be read at morning and evening worship. Even the superstition of servants could scarcely have impressed the imagination that had not wakened in its earliest dawn as yet. Month by month the same story was repeated, always with reluctance, which yielded only to the pressure of entreaties—and with such seeming reverence as made the hearer solemn, too. Did it hold any connection with the trance of two years before? Was there an overlapping of the two worlds across the border of thread, upon which for so many hours the little spirit was balancing? Had she then a vision, the reminiscence of which came dimly back upon the dawning intellect—straining itself through earthly images given by the senses, and made somewhat grotesque by the unnatural commingling? Who can tell? It is enough that the keeper of the gate has at last let her in—that she walks with him in white—that she looks with the "pure in heart" upon the face of the King; and may God in holy covenant grant, that we may all sit in the golden chairs which her infant eye saw placed for father and mother and the other five.

The years rolled on—years of careful parental training and years of physical and mental growth—some of them years of frightful civil war, which laid the cares of age upon the heart of youth and made even children men. At length she stood before us in the maturity of early womanhood, the pride and joy of those by whom she was tenderly loved. But it is only since she left us that we begin to put things together, and better understand a character which was before somewhat a puzzle to explain. With the style of beauty which fascinates in youth and becomes queenly when rounded into the

proportions of age, it lay upon her as the
sunbeam lies upon the unconscious flower.
The thought could not be put in her from
without ; and every chance note of admira-
tion glanced off, leaving no more trace
than of the arrow through the air.   The
sceptre of maidenly conquest and rule lay
untouched at her feet.   The ambition of
youth and beauty to assert the power of
both, slumbered in her heart.   It was not
so much indifference, as a total unconsciousness of its presence.   Would a sense
of its power have broken upon her at last ?
Who knows ?   But she carried up to God
a heart in its virgin freshness, which the
voice of flattery had never been able to soil.

There was another paradox in her character.   Thrown into the bosom of a large
society, and commingling with persons of
every class, she was indisposed to be drawn
into any of its eddies.   Beyond two or
three cherished friendships, no amount of
kindly force could push her out to take her
place as a woman in the world.   Her love
was concentrated upon her home ; and the

ties of sister and daughter were all the bonds on earth she cared to recognize. Even in this narrow sphere her love was unobtrusive. Averse from the caresses of others, and tendering no endearments from herself, it was felt as one feels the light— by an ever genial presence. It was only in the occasional emergencies breaking up the routine of family life, that the crust of reserve gave way and revealed the passionate depths to which that quiet silent love did reach. The same individuality was as clearly defined in the intellectual, as in the emotional sphere. So far from merely reflecting the influences which bore upon her, a trenchant criticism would often betray the independence of her own observations of life. And these, though never obtruded, were not kept under the same seal of secretiveness with utterances that might savor of sentiment. In a word, few persons so young were more self-contained ; which, perhaps, gives the key to all that seemed so surprising in the dying experience presently to be recorded.

How early one so reticent began to be interested in the subject of personal religion, perhaps even she herself could not have told.   Certainly it would not betray itself to others by any transient emotion, which she was able so perfectly to control. It would not escape through any utterance of the lips, until conviction had pretty well ripened into fixed religious principle. She was one to fight the battle out alone, until the time should come to declare the issue. The first disclosure was made to the sister next above her in age.   Lying across the bed, the two talked together of a sudden death which had recently occurred :

"As for myself," said K——, "I would rather die from consumption than from any other disease."

Her sister, in surprise, exclaimed :

"Why, K——!"

"Yes," was the response, "because it is a lingering disease, and more free from pain than most others."

"Perhaps so," replied the sister, "to the invalid herself, but not to friends who watch around the bed."

"That is true," was the answer; and the subject was dropped—but not until the faithful sister sought to bear it down in a close application to the conscience. As might have been expected, however, the appeal was received in respectful silence, but the silence of complete reserve. Soon after a little note was pinned on the table cushion, reading after this tenor:

"Dear G——, I wish you would talk with me on a certain subject; you know what I mean."

Even a crumpled note must bear the impress of her character: a direct brevity that would waste no words, and the use of an enigma to veil, if not to suppress, all sentiment. The germinating seed was now ready to burst through the soil, and come to the light and air. The requested interview revealed the fact of a soul that had passed through its travail, and was resting quietly upon the peace of the Gospel. In October, 1869, she united with the Church of God upon the profession of her faith and

hope; and sat the next Sabbath at the
Supper of the Lamb.

The last sad chapter of this story alone
remains. In the Autumn of 1870 a hard
bronchial cough became the precursor of
the insidious disease which does its work
so surely, sapping a frail constitution from
beneath. With obstinate defiance it re-
sisted the highest medical skill. No pal-
liatives soothed it; all attempts at cure it
simply mocked. Travel was advised; and
the summer months of 1871 were spent in
an extended tour through the North and
Canada. Not the first indication of improvement was perceived, and we knew
just how it must end. But none dreamed
how soon that end would come. With
waning strength, indeed, still the fatigues
of travel were borne with comparative
comfort till the faces of the party were
turned homeward. With effort the journey
was continued; and about the middle of
September we reached a place that seemed
like home, in the house of the grandmother. Here the whole system gave

way, and she became alarmingly ill. Three weeks of careful nursing were required before the case yielded to medical treatment. She was now entirely prostrate, her strength reduced to the feebleness of infancy. It was a gracious reprieve, suspending the issue long enough to renew the journey to our own abode. Borne in the arms and reclining on beds extemporized in the cars, we succeeded by easy stages in reaching home, on the 6th of October. She was borne in the arms to her chamber, from which she was carried in exactly three weeks to the tomb. There was no reason in the nature of her disease, proverbially so lingering, for this early termination, except the unconquerable loathing of all food—which, undoubtedly, was a feature of the malady itself. Her case was in this respect precisely similar to that of her sister, whose death has already been recorded; who, in the same degree, turned with disgust from every solicitation of the appetite. Though distinctly admonished that the preservation of life depended upon enriching the blood, which nutrition alone could effect; and notwithstanding that she summoned all the energies of her will to overcome this unnatural repugnance, every effort failed. Delicacies of every description and food that would have tempted an epicure, lay untouched at her side; and it was evident that she must die of sheer inanition, as much as from the disease itself. The jealous apprehensions of her faithful mother were the first to realize the fact, and with almost prophetic instinct assigned the limit beyond which her endurance could not pass. She died within the period thus by anticipation fixed. This mother, too, was the first to break the reserve hitherto maintained, and sounded the first warning to the dying child.

It fell in the gentlest form of suggestion, and spoke of the disappointment we all felt that the cough got no better, and expressed the fear that she would never recover. She was also asked if she would like her father to pray with and for her; to which

a cordial assent was given. From this time
onward family worship was held morning
and evening in her chamber; and the poor
sufferer was borne upon the faith of all our
hearts to the Mercy-seat above. In the
evening of the same day the warning was
enforced by her sister G——, who generally watched with her when the family
was at meals, and embraced those oppor-
tunities for confidential conversations. She
said :

"K——, you do not know how it pains
us to see you so sick and weak: do you
know how sick you are?"

"No," was the reply, "not if it is what
the doctor calls it: in one respect I am
worse, I cannot eat."

"I am afraid you are very sick," replied
the sister; "if it should be God's will to
take you, would you be alarmed?"

"No," was the steady response.

G—— then resumed:

"After all, death is nothing to a believer."

The conversation glanced from this direct

application, and they spoke of a friend who had recently died of the same disease, and generally of how terrible it was to die if unprepared to meet God.

"I think," said the sufferer, ' that dreadful weakness that comes just before death, must be awful."

"It is not always so," was the reply; " in sister F——'s case, for instance, how strong she became before she died!"

These suggestive and preliminary conversations prepared the way for a more definite announcement of her critical condition on the following Monday, October 23d. The stern duty was laid upon the father to cut away all ground of hope from his darling child, and to open to her the certainty of her approaching doom. Would she be able to bear it? Evidently she had rallied to hope upon the supposition that her disease was not incurable. With the extinction of all hope, would not an immediate collapse ensue? And what if terror and alarm should seize her spirit, and his **words hasten the dreaded catastrophe?**

Thoughts like these flitted through his mind, like birds of evil omen. It was as though the patriarchal Abraham must lift the sacrificial knife over the beloved Isaac again. Yet the poor girl must not be suffered to make the dreadful plunge wholly in the dark. The highest Christian love pleaded that she might at least be allowed to "gather up her feet in her bed" ere she left us. Breaking his ground cautiously, he asked :

"K——, do you know how sick you really are? and do you not think sometimes that it is impossible for you to recover?"

"No, I do not think that I am so very sick; if I could only eat, that is my trouble."

"But, my daughter, do you not see that this is a part of your disease, and the worst part of it, too?"

She was silent, and he continued :

"My darling, it is best you should know the whole truth about yourself: it is now certain that you have consumption; hitherto your lungs have been in what the

doctors call a state of consolidation or
hardening; now they are beginning to
break down, and will go entirely in the
course of time. You may linger as many
do, or you may be taken away at almost
any moment. Tell me, daughter, does
this alarm you ? Are you afraid to die ?"

With a superb courage, without the
moistening of an eye or the quivering of a
muscle, she heard her doom; and folding
her hands on her breast, simply said :

" I am ready."

" Is your hope fixed simply upon Christ
as your Redeemer, my child?"

" Yes, I have nothing else to trust to
but that," was the reply which closed
the interview. It would have been comforting to have drawn her out in the details
of Christian experience, but in compassion
it was spared. Even this brief conversation was at the expense of much suffering
from unutterable exhaustion and the inces-
sant cough which speaking only irritated
and increased. In the evening of the same
day she repeated to a younger sister the

substance of what had been said about her physical condition, and added:

"But I am so weak that I cannot talk. Father is going to have prayer with me."

A little later she inquired when a certain lady was to be married, alluding to an engagement which would take her father from home.

"On the 16th of November," was the answer; but father will not go now, as you are so sick."

She rejoined:

"It may be all over with me before then."

G—— exclaimed:

"K——, how can you talk about it so calmly?"

"Well," she replied, "I don't want to be frightened about it, when the time comes; and I hope I won't."

"No, you will not be," the sister added, "God will give you strength for it; don't you remember how sister dreaded it, and how calm she was when the time came?"

With a sudden lighting up of the countenance, the dying girl exclaimed:

"Oh! she will be there to meet me, won't she?"

On Tuesday, October 24th, the doctor paid a long visit; and called G—— out on leaving, to warn her against sleeping with the patient; as she was just in that condition to communicate the disease. That night K—— said to her sister:

"What did the doctor call you out for? Was it to say that my lungs were affected?"

"Yes, K——, he did."

"Well, he need not have minded saying that before me; I am not surprised."

She then inquired about her sister's case, who had died:

"Did sister cough and spit, as I do?"

"Yes, just the same."

"Then I think I ought to have a pallet all to myself. I always thought my left side affected; and asked ————— if ever I had anything the matter with my lungs, would it be the left one, and he said yes. Now I understand why sister never would sleep with her face towards us."

After awhile she inquired whether it was

her sister's right or left lung that was affected, and was told it was her right lung.

On Wednesday, October 25th, a note was read to her from a kind Christian friend, expressing sympathy with her sufferings, and asking her to tell her mother or any one else for him, whether the Saviour was precious to her. At the close she simply said : "Tell him yes." G—— then asked if she would not send a message to her Sabbath-school class; as one from her now would do more good than a thousand from herself. She replied :

"Yes, but make a message for me—I can't."

"Shall I tell them, then, that the young die as well as the old, and let your case be a warning to them?"

"Yes," was the answer, "let this be a warning to them not to put off preparing for death ; for they may be in too much pain, or else too weak."

On Thursday, October 26th, about three in the afternoon, she had a sinking spell, so that we thought her dying. When she

had a little revived, her father said,
"K——, you are very weak." She
nodded assent, being too feeble to speak.
"Is the Saviour very precious to you, my
child?" To which assent was given in the
same way as before. She appeared to rally
from this prostration, and grew bighter
with the advancing day, but coughing in-
cessantly and unable to bring up the
phlegm from her throat.

As evening deepened into night, by a
sort of common understanding and without
conference, the entire family remained up;
no one thought of disrobing for sleep. The
unexpressed fear lay like a shadow upon
every face, that the hour of her departure
was at hand. The instinctive prophecy
was fulfilled: those beautiful eyes never
again greeted the rising sun. About two
o'clock in the morning of Friday, October
27th, the final change was indicated by a
degree of nervousness which led to the request that her limbs might be rubbed.
When this had been continued some time
she arrested it, saying, "I think I will go

to sleep now ; I would like to, if I could."
We sat around in silence, vainly hoping
that she might enjoy even a refreshing
doze. As this was wooed in vain, her
father said :

"Daughter, is the Saviour near you?"

To which she answered in almost a
deprecatory tone :

"Yes, sir ; but I am—too weak—to say
—a thing."

All joined in chorus :

"We know it, don't talk."

An hour or two later, thinking the servants would feel hurt if not allowed to
come in and look once more upon the
living face, at the mother's request they
were wakened and invited in, if they so
desired. They all gathered at the summons, and the melancholy group stood
weeping around the bed. Her eye ranged
around the circle, resting in turn upon
each. The father spake :

"You see, K——, we are all here."

"Yes."

Remaining quiet for some time, she was

seized with another sinking spell, and cried :
" Brandy—quick—something to eat." A
little piece of cracker was handed to her,
which she began to eat with an impatient
haste that smote our hearts with its mock-
ery. The poor girl who had turned for
weeks from food as the object of supreme
disgust, now in the last battle for life was
munching almost ravenously a piece of dry
bread to fend off the awful weakness she
had so much dreaded as the precursor of
death. Reviving a little from the stimulus
administered, broken words fell from her
lips, but in a voice too faint to be caught
She then endeavored to turn upon her side,
but could not without assistance. " It is
so hard to sleep; I think I will sleep first
and eat afterwards." The icy touch was
upon her limbs. Gathering the coverlet up
to her neck, a slight sign of aberration
manifested itself in the cry, " Take this
cold cup away." Placing her hand at the
same time into her bosom, she said, " I
am almost asleep now." Ah, yes, but it
was the sleep from which none ever wake

until the Resurrection morn. Presently raising her finger and pointing it towards the window, she exclaimed: "THERE!" Who can tell the import of that typical gesture? As the curtain rolls up before the dying, do they see aught beyond— catching glimpses of the Spirit world to which the eye of sense is closed? Soon after, her face lighted up with a strange radiance, and the words "Welcome, wel- come," fell twice upon the ear. Her sis- ter bending over her asked: "Did you say welcome, K——?" To which she answered: "Yes, welcome!" Ah! was this the greeting of a ransomed spirit to the shining ones she saw upon the banks of the cold river she was crossing, waiting to convey her home? The mysteries of a dying hour are known only to those who are passing through them, and the secret is too precious to be breathed into mortal ears. Once more it was asked of her, "Is Jesus very near to you now?" and the head bowed in quiet assent. The eyes began to wear that stony look where speculation is lost. The father moved his fingers rapidly before them, and they did not wink.   He bowed over her—" Do you know me, K——?" One slight movement showed that consciousness, though fading fast, was not quite gone.   To test this further, he asked the mother to put the same question.   She hesitated an instant, saying, " Do not disturb her, she is almost gone ; " but yielded at length.   " K——, do you know mother?"   But in that brief instant the curtain had fallen; the senses were closed against all approach; and gently as an infant falls to sleep on its mother's breast, she, our darling, fell asleep in Jesus.   Just as the morning light was pencilling the horizon, and the early dawn was waking up a sleeping world, she awoke where there is no more night, in the world of everlasting day.

In comparing this experience with that of the preceding sketch, the impression is deepened as to the influence of natural disposition upon the religious life.   In the

the elder sister, Divine Grace had to con-
tend with timidity and self-distrust ; which
were overcome only at the last moment,
and then without any marked sign of triumph. In the present case, a nature more
self-reliant afforded an easier conquest of
the fear of death. No small portion of our
discomfort arises from not taking into account our constitutional temperament, in
the attempt to analyze our Christian state.
All Christian experience cannot be run in
the same mould. The elements may be
the same, but the combinations will vary ;
and the forces to be overcome will be different. In the development of the spiritual
life the Holy Ghost may be expected to
recognize the original traits which stamp
on each believer an individuality of his
own. Upon the preservation of this individuality depends largely the value of the
testimony, which each shall deliver to the
glory of the grace that each may have enjoyed. It may be that the blending of
these different experiences, like the
different chords in music, shall constitute

the harmony of song forever heard in the Upper Temple.

Even this does not exhaust the lesson taught in these two sketches. There is the exhibition of the Divine Sovereignty in shaping the whole character and life, from the cradle to the grave, for uses known only to Himself in the eternal world. The natural traits themselves, the discipline of Providence under which these are developed, and the operations of grace by which these in turn are modified—all are of one piece in the Divine plan. The blending of these factors in the one result was designed from the beginning. In the lives protracted through three and four-score years, the web is too complex for us to distinguish the lines where these various influences meet and blend. But in these early deaths the process is more easily traced. Why, for example, should this young girl be endowed with rare personal charms, without the ambition even to appear in society, unless the Lord was thus removing a snare from her feet, and preparing her for the early sacrifice to which she was called? How assuring the truth that we and our times are all in His hands, from life's dawn to its close!

But the special lesson taught in this bereavement, is the mystery that lies in life and in death. Whence come these shadows upon our earthly path, from the realities of the Upper World? And whence these glimpses of the Heavenly State, which sometimes shed its radiance upon the face of the dying saint? Undoubtedly we must abide solely by the teachings of the inspired Word; and in deference to its reserve on all these points, we must repress the vain imaginings which we are prone to indulge. But with God and Heaven in immediate prospect, and with the Holy Ghost within the soul preparing it for the early enjoyment of both, is it strange that a foretaste should be afforded of that spiritual world to which it is akin?

The lines herewith appended seem to harmonize with the sketch given above:

" It lies around us like a cloud,
   A world we do not see;
   Yet the sweet closing of an eye
   May bring us there to be.

" Its gentle breezes fan our cheek;
   Amid our worldly cares.
   Its gentle voices whisper love,
   And mingle with our prayers.

" Sweet hearts around us throb and beat,
   Sweet helping hands are stirred,
   And palpitates the veil between
   With breathings almost heard.

" The silence—awful, sweet and calm—
   They have no power to break;
   For mortal words are not for them
   To utter or partake.

" So thin, so soft, so sweet they glide,
   So near to press they seem—
   They seem to lull us to our rest,
   And melt into our dream.

" And in the hush of rest they bring
   'Tis easy now to see,
   How lovely, and how sweet a pass,
   The hour of death may be.

" To close the eye, and close the ear,
   Wrapped in a trance of bliss,
   And gently dream in loving arms
   To swoon to that—from this."

IV.

" My Father, say, must this pet lamb be given ?
  Oh, Thou hast many such, dear Lord in Heaven,
  And a soft voice said, ' Nobly hast thou striven ;
      But—peace, be still.' "

Within fifteen months we were called to
the surrender of another, the youngest of
our fold, who had just passed her seven-
teenth birthday. From early infancy she
was characterized by unusual gentleness of
disposition, which became more conspicu-
ous as her character was developed. There
was little occasion for parental discipline ;
and never except for trivial faults arising
only from the general imperfection of human nature. The severest punishment was
withholding from her the manifestations of
love, upon which her young heart was accustomed to feed. Her manner was self-
contained and quiet ; so that whilst affec-
tionate and confiding, she was not obtru-

sively demonstrative. Her love for others
was displayed rather in a thoughtful con-
sideration for their convenience and comfort ; and the sacrifice of her own inclina-
tions was so constant that it seemed to be
the prompting of an instinct. Her love
for her mother mounted into worship ; and
the quiet, simple expression of it was often
touching in its pathos.

Her constitution was always delicate,
rendering her education necessarily irregu-
lar. The tenderness of her eyes prevented
her for weeks together from opening a
book, making her dependent largely on
oral instruction. In this way she acquired
a complete knowledge of English grammar ;
and could analyze the most complex passage in poetry, without having traced with
the eye a single rule of syntax. She thus
acquired a remarkable power of concentration and abstraction, which was of incal-
culable advantage in her later education.
Up to the moment the hand of disease
arrested her studies, her lessons were
learned by simply hearing them read ; and

were recited with such accuracy as secured a high grade of scholarship in her class. Her mind was not rapid in its movement, but her retention of knowledge was perfect ; and her habitual thoughtfulness incorporated it with the substance of her intellectual being. She gave the promise of ripening into a woman of solid attainments, notwithstanding the disadvantages under which she labored ; for thoughtfulness was equally with her an intellectual and a moral trait.

She always seemed to me, to be one of those children who are sanctified from the birth. Her whole life was so conspicuously ruled by principle, and her affections were so determined by conscience, that we never felt anxiety about her spiritual state. Her connection with the church was formed, however, at an early period—on the 7th of June, 1871, when fifteen and a half years old. It has never been our habit to press the subject of joining the church upon our children at an early age. Our aim has been to bring a quiet and constant influ-

ence to bear upon them ; and then to wait for
the spontaneous development of religious
feeling under the power of the Holy Spirit.
One Sabbath, a little before the date mentioned above, I happened to be alone with
her while returning from church : thinking
it a good opportunity to sound her upon
the subject, I said :

"M——, I do not talk much with you
about religion ; but you must not suppose
this springs from indifference.   I often
think of it, and pray for your conversion.
You are no longer a child, and fully understand your duty and the way of salvation
by Jesus Christ ; and it would make your
mother and myself very happy to know
that you had fully accepted Him in your
heart."

I was not wholly taken by surprise,
though scarcely expecting the answer to
be so full and satisfactory :

"Father, I have long desired to unite
with the church, for I do love and trust
my Saviour."

Upon being questioned how far back

these religious feelings could be traced, it turned out—as I have anticipated in this narrative—that she could assign no period for their commencement. She had never known the time when her heart did not turn to God as her Portion, and to Jesus as her Redeemer. Like Lydia, the Lord had "opened her heart," and she had been drawn by a single thread of love into the Kingdom. Not a shadow of doubt rested upon her mind, or upon ours; and she went down into the Valley of the Shadow of Death without one quiver of fear; for to love and to trust were wrought into her whole being, and she had no conception of anything else.

I approach now the record of her fatal illness, which lasted altogether but a single year. She was taken down with pneumonia on the 3d of February, 1872. The attack was severe, and blisters were freely applied to relieve the pain; but it yielded under treatment. Though exceedingly delicate, she seemed so far recovered that her school duties were resumed. Our

apprehensions were too easily allayed, the
disease was by no means conquered. One
morning after breakfast she complained of
tightness across her chest, adding that she
had felt it for several days ; but did not
speak of it, hoping it would wear away.
She was immediately examined by her
brother-in-law, who said, "M——, lay
down your books and go to your chamber ;" and she succumbed at once under
another attack of pneumonia. From this
also she rallied, so as to move about her
chamber as an invalid. The conviction
was, however, lodged in her mind, that
the struggle with disease was to end in
death.   Its grasp was so tenacious, it
would scarcely leave without depositing
the germ which must end in dissolution.
On the first of May, as she retired to bed,
she exclaimed :

"Well, here I am on the first of May,
and I will be here on the first day of June,
and then of July ; and so on to November,
when I will drop off!"

In this prediction, however, she was

mistaken. Before November the traces of pneumonia had disappeared; but the evidence was only too certain of that wasting consumption which had carried off her two sisters before her eyes. We had come to know its signs too well to be ourselves deceived by any false hopes for her. It was as yet in its early stage; and though unquestionably doomed, in that beautiful Autumnal month she was able to take easy walks with her sisters in the streets, and several rides with us in the open country beyond the paved and dusty city. Her testimony was constantly repeated that this was only a respite, and with it an unquestioning submission to the Divine will:

"Though I am better, yet we do not know how it will end; we do not know what is best for us—may be if I should get well, in after life I might regret I had not died at this time."

In one of her short walks a funeral procession passed by. It threw a shade over her heart as she said in her simple way: "What little difference it makes in the world."

Ah ! this thought of being forgotten by
the living, is it not one of the pangs of the
dying ? Does it not throw a deeper gloom
over the darkness of the grave ? In the
anticipation of it, Kirk White speaks
mournfully thus :

> " I shall sink
> As sinks a stranger in the crowded streets
> Of busy London ; some short bustle's caused,
> A few inquiries, and the crowds close in—
> And all's forgotten."

Our darling F—— paused once, like
this young sister, an invalid in her evening
walk, as a funeral passed—and half-gaily,
half-sadly, said :

" So will my funeral pass ; and one will
say, ' Whose funeral is that ? ' the answer
will be, ' F—— P——'s ; ' and then there
will be a shaking of the head, ' Poor girl !
she is dead then ; ' and they will pass on
and forget."

Ah ! my child, there are hearts in which
you cannot be forgotten. The tomb stones
bear the names of four, who once made
this home so happy ; but the lasting marble
will not preserve the imperishable memory,

like these living hearts that feel each day the pain of parting afresh. This must last till the sting is plucked away in the joyful meeting above.

During the illness of this dear child the conversations were chiefly conducted by her older sister, who was her constant companion. This duty was devolved upon her in the belief that the expression of her feelings would be more free and full to the sister with whom she was on such easy terms, than to ourselves. From notes carefully kept at the time, the following statement was compiled:

My first conversation with her (says G——) were on the 3d of August. I began by saying:

"M——, you do not know what a lesson in patience you are to me all the time; do you never feel impatient?"

"No," was the reply.

"It requires more faith," I continued, "to die young than old; don't you think so?"

"Yes," was the reply; "I thought

after K——'s death, that it did not make any difference how soon it came ; but then I was in perfect health, and this makes a great difference. I suppose I ought not to give up all hope ; but there were a great many ' ifs ' in the way, and I know I have not improved since then."

The last allusion was to a remark made some time before by the physician, that if this and that could be brought about, she might still get well. The conversation between the two sisters is resumed :

" Well, M——, how do you feel about it ? Are you willing to have it end either way ? "

" Yes, I hope I am," was the answer.

On the first of September, continues her sister, I was telling her about the Communion season just passed, and from that we got to speaking about the Resurrection.

" Don't you suppose," she asked, "that the spirits recognize each other before they get their bodies ?"

" Undoubtedly," answered the sister.

" It all seems so strange, sometimes I

get completely lost when I think about death. Here we live on from day to day, and to think of it all coming to an end— nothing more—it is so strange."

September 5th—

"You do not know," she said to her sister, "how I shuddered to-day when the doctor remarked that I might live ten years in this condition. I would a great deal rather die. Life has no enjoyment to one in my condition: then, too, I would be a burden to all around me."

"You will never be a burden," was the reply; "you are so patient and cheerful that it is a pleasure to wait on you; never feel that way about it."

Resuming her thoughts, she said:

"What might not happen in ten years! Why, mother might die, and father, too. They say my lung is hardening, it has not begun to soften yet. I never expect to get well; sometimes when I am a little better, I hope; and then I feel may be I ought not to want to get well—I do not know what is best."

"Yes," her sister replied, "death is not the worst thing that can happen. I would rather be in my grave than have to bear what some women do."

"Yes, indeed," she rejoined, "I think about it all the time. I know it has got to be borne; it may be nearer now than I think."

"Well, M——, how do you feel about it? Do you shrink from death?"

"No, I do not feel afraid to die."

"Having seen our sisters go so calmly," it was suggested, "makes us dread it less."

"Yes, it does make a great difference;" and then she added:

"I am so glad it is I, and not you or sister M——: you both have ties that I have not."

"But, M——, in a little while you would have had the same ties."

"Ah, yes, but that is all in the future."

September 7th she opened the conversation with her sister:

"Brother J—— examined me yester-day—I asked him to do it : I want to know how my lung is going. He says if I had a strong constitution I might live a long time ; but I know he does not think as the doctor does."

She referred to K——'s death about a year ago, in that indefinite way peculiar to her—avoiding the mention of her name :

"That night I wondered who would be the next to go ; and then I thought it was eight years since sister F—— died, and that is a long time. It may be eight years before another is taken. I can't help filling up when I think of leaving you all."

October 2d—

To-day she said she was done with life, and hoped she was ready to die : she thought she was, and hoped she would feel so when the time came. She then exacted of me (continues the sister) the promise that I would tell her when the doctor gave up all hope of her recovery ; saying she did not wish the fact to be kept from her.

On the 20th of November she came down stairs for the last time. As she retired to bed that night, she said to her mother: "I am here now for good."

On Christmas day, her sister M—— gave birth to a babe, and the invalid was assisted out of bed, and with much effort tottered to her sister's chamber. When the little infant was placed in her arms, she said, "I never expected to hold this baby." Upon returning to her own bed, the little stranger was carried and laid at her side. that she might look at him. After this she never left her couch, and spoke but little. It may be mentioned here, that, solely with a view to her gratification, the infant was baptized on the 12th of January in her chamber—the last solemn rite of the Church in which she participated.

January 30th, 1873—

At night she called for her mother, and said :

"I only wanted to say to you that I think it will be all over before morning."

"Well, M——, do you still feel that

same sweet trust that you are going right
to the Saviour?"

"Yes, ma'am," was the answer.

"And you will not be there alone, my
daughter."

"No, no," answered she, "there are
three there already."

"Have you any request to make, my
darling?"

"No; you can keep the coffin open
until the hour of the funeral, and then
close it."

M——, the elder sister, exclaimed:

"Oh, M——, don't talk about that!"
She turned and asked:

"What was it you asked me to tell you
about, sister G——?"

"About what, M——?" not recalling
what she referred to.

"You asked me long ago to tell you
something when I was dying."

"O, yes," she replied; "if sister and
K——should come to meet you."

The following morning her mother said,
"Well, daughter, you did not leave us

last night as you thought you would;"
to which her only answer was, "No,
ma'am."

January 31st—

She lay with her eyes closed, only opening them when addressed, or to fix them
on her mother, whom she loved with an
affection approaching idolatry. So completely was she withdrawn from earth that
a fire directly across the street, with all the
noise and confusion of the engines at play,
did not attract her notice. During this
long illness she manifested no desire to
converse with her mother on the subject of
her departure. The great pang in dying
was the separation from her which it involved; and she turned from its contem-
plation as too painful. With her father
she was less reserved; but he was so satisfied of her preparation for the great change,
that he was indisposed to vex her weakness
with frequent conversations. Still these
were occasionally held from the beginning
of her sickness till its close, always result-
ing in the unvarying statement of her

assured and peaceful hope in the Redeemer, whom she embraced as "all her salvation and her desire." There was nothing for her, as for us, but to wait quietly the execution of God's resistless and holy will. Alas! we knew not the severity of the test to which this submission was to be subjected.

February 1st, 1873—

As the day was rising to its noon, it became apparent that the shadows of the Valley were darkening about her. At two in the afternoon, a weeping group was gathered around her bed; there was but a single prayer left to be breathed on her behalf—it was for a gentle release.

"Oh," cried the mother, "if she could only be spared the agony of suffocation!"

" She lies peacefully," replied the father, "in a few moments she will be at rest forever."

Just then she turned her head upon the pillow. The movement was fatal—a single cough—the child was strangling!!! The father leaped upon the bed and raised the

skeleton frame in his arms : only a single
cry of distress from those bloodless lips—
one despairing look at each of the watching circle—one feeble clutch of the thin
fingers at the neck of her dress—and all
was over !   "Oh, my God !" burst from
the mother's breaking heart, as the child
expired in the father's arms.

Oh, Death, was there no mercy in thy
pitiless bosom, that at the last, like a beast
of prey, thou must leap upon that wasted
form ; and with ruffian violence wrench
away the young life which she was yielding
so gently up to God !

Be still, my soul ! It is the most solemn
lesson Providence has ever taught thee of
THE AWFULNESS OF SIN.   She, the gentlest
of them all, whom the Lord sanctified even
from the womb ; who never by word or
sign betrayed the patience which possessed
her soul—the most like an angel of all this
sinning race : because the Lord loved her
and showed how fondly He had placed her
in His bosom—just because of this, in His
dreadful sovereignty, He chose to stamp

upon this gentle one the seal of His hatred of sin, when reduced even to the least.

Thou art our martyr, M——! God called thee to honor Him by a life of sweet obedience from the cradle; and then to bear the seal of His consuming holiness in the agony of Death.

Blessed witness for thy God, in living and in dying! Thou art now beneath the Throne, where all the martyrs are; and the memory of thee is to us a constant call from Heaven.

> " We stood beside the river,
>   Whence all our souls must go;
>   Bearing a loved one in our arms,
>   Our hearts repeating the alarms
>   That came across the river;
>   And saw the sun decline in mist,
>   That rose until her brow it kissed,
>   And left it cold as snow.
>
> " Watching beside the river,
>   With every ebb and flow,
>   Fond hopes within our hearts would spring,
>   Until another warning ring
>   Came o'er the fearful river.
>   We saw the flush, the brightness fade,
>   The loving lips looked grieved and sad,
>   The white hands whiter grow.

" Standing by the river,
  We closed the weary eyes,
  In Jesus' arms we laid her down,
  A lovely jewel for His crown.
  He bore her through the river,
  And clothed her in a robe so white,
  Too beautiful for mortal sight,
  And took her to the skies."

V.

"O, one after one they flew away,
Far up to the heavenly blue,
To the better country, the upper day,
And—I wish I was going, too."

The cup of sorrow was not yet full.
During two and thirty years, four of the
six whom the Lord had given to us were
taken hence; and now one of the two left
must be surrendered to Him, whose claim
was more perfect than our own. The
daughter who was introduced in the preceding sketch, as leading her younger
sister sweetly down into the dark Valley,
is now called to descend herself into its
deepest gloom. The following is the
record of her illness and death.

From early childhood she gave indica-
tions of a decided character, which did not
fail to be fulfilled in after years. Her dis-
tinguishing trait, at this early period, was
the almost entire absence of selfishness

and wilfulness. Her submission to parental
authority was prompt and easy; and there
was, in her youthful sports, such a surrender of her own preferences and tastes
to those of her companions, as filled us
with surprise. This spirit of self-abnegation
marked her whole career in life; which, in
later years, might have been ascribed to
an instinctive prudence and discretion—or
else to the influence of a careful Christian
training. But it was an original trait ex-
hibited with as much clearness and power
in childhood as in mature years; and it
stood in such marked contrast with the
usual self-will and waywardness of the
young, as sometimes to suggest the thought
of God's special grace as its source. The
disclosure of her religious experience, when
brought into the Kingdom, convinced us,
however, that it was a natural, though
unusual, trait; and that she could not be
classed with her sister, whose decease has
just been presented, as one renewed from
the beginning. It made us feel that God
had committed to our care a very precious

child, who, under judicious management, would certainly expand into a noble woman. What rendered this self-denying and yielding temper the more remarkable, was a positiveness of character, which discriminated her gentleness from a negative easiness that can be turned and moulded by the stronger will of those around her. I desire to emphasize this co-ordinate and qualifying trait, as it early arrested my attention and made her an object of study. There is, perhaps, no better term by which to describe it, than the general one employed above. The word *positiveness*, vague as it may appear, expresses the idea of an all-pervading quality that gave tone and depth to her character, without impairing its softness. It never degenerated into wilfulness or stubbornness, but assumed the form of a quiet and amiable decision. I shall have to signalize two occasions, at least, on which this trait was conspicuously revealed; but from the first it ran like a scarlet thread through her entire history.

This combination of qualities made up an interesting problem, which I was never able fully to resolve. If constitutionally unselfish, ever postponing her own enjoyment to that of others, it was not due to any deficiency of will; which any one could discern lying back, and hidden like the spinal column in the human body. Those familiar with her in later life recognized her as a person of assured convictions and great tenacity of purpose. She never was, either as child or woman, an easy-going facile person. However inclined modestly to defer to others whom she considered intelligent and wise, she framed her own independent judgments, and did not hold them lightly in her grasp. This amiable independence of thought and character, was one of the points of resemblance to her mother; whose quiet decision of mind and temper has made her so invaluable a counsellor, a helpful as well as a loving companion to me.

When about thirteen and a half years old, the subject of this sketch, with her sister just above her in age, united with the church. I was not surpised when she announced to me her interest on the subject of personal religion. I looked for her to glide into the communion of the church, as soon as mature enough to take in the import of such a step. I was not prepared, however, for the revelation which she actually made. With her characteristic decision she took me one evening into the piazza, saying, "Father, I want to talk with you alone." She then disclosed a struggle in her little bosom, to which I listened with unbounded astonishment. This immature girl, who I thought had only to wake to full self-knowledge in order to find herself within the Kingdom, had been battling for weeks with almost every form of skepticism and infidelity. She had never read a line in any book which suggested these difficulties. She had never talked with any one infected with these notions: her intercourse had been exclusively with persons who reverenced and loved the Bible. And then, these matters

seemed so far beyond and above her years.
How came this child to be agitated with
doubts about the being and personality of
God—about the immortality of the soul—
whether death was not the final sleep—
whether all religion was not a mere superstition—the Bible a fiction—Jesus Christ
an impostor—Eternity, the Judgment,
Heaven and Hell, mere crazy dreams such
as come into the mind of some half-frenzied
poet? The battle was well-nigh fought,
when she uncovered the secret to me; and
perhaps all that was needed to complete
the victory, was just to tell the story of
her temptations. But as I listened, I felt
that the Devil could teach a child much
that was beyond her years. It was, at
least, intensely interesting, as an instance
of precocious thought, to follow her mental processes as she developed these various speculations, and formed her own
independent refutation of them. The result was that she settled down into an intelligent belief in Christianity, which was
never afterwards shaken by a solitary doubt.

The next important step in her history
was her marriage in May, 1873; which
took place at a time of great domestic
sorrow, being only three months after the
sad death of our martyr, M———, already
recorded. It afforded opportunity, however, for displaying the universal esteem
and love in which she was held. The
church in which the marriage was solemn-
ized, was elaborately and exquisitely fes-
tooned and decorated with flowers by a
multitude of loving hands; and a grateful
surprise was furnished us by those who
combined to make the occasion one of
gladness, and to show the appreciation in
which this dear child was held—giving us
more pleasure in the memory of it, now
that she has passed into the Paradise above
where the flowers bloom and never fade.

On the 29th of June, 1874, she gave
birth to her little babe, left to us a legacy
of love. From this sickness she never
rallied, and the fatal disease was soon developed which took her away. Her health
had not been previously robust. For two

or three years she had been troubled with
a bronchial affection, which, united with
dyspeptic symptoms, had often excited
apprehension that she might be called
eventually to follow her sisters, whose decline had been indicated by similar local
disorders.   Through the remainder of that
year the disease seemed to be held at bay.
Her appetite was sustained, the food easily
digested, and daily rides into the open
country were enjoyed.   But these appear-
ances were deceptive, and the fatal consumption was secretly sapping the system
within.   From the 4th to the 26th of
January, 1875, I was separated from her,
being called to a distance in the perform-
ance of certain ecclesiastical duties. Upon
my return it was only too manifest that
her case was hopeless, and that her departure could not long be postponed.   It
became now an imperative duty to break
through the reserve hitherto maintained,
and as gently as possible to intimate the
change that was inevitable. So long as a
particle of hope remained of even possible

recovery, we had been careful to sustain her spirits by cheerful anticipation of the future. Confronted now by the certainty of death, Christian faithfulness required that she should not be taken unawares.

January 29th, 1875—

On this morning I determined to know the worst from her physician, who said that she had evidently lost ground, but might rally again with a favorable turn in the weather; but that there was no chance for her recovery. Upon going up to her chamber, I found that she had drawn out of him a similar opinion.

"I have at last," she said, "gotten from the doctor a candid statement of my case."

I mentioned frankly what he had just said to me; but went on to speak hopefully of what might take place in her favor even yet. About five o'clock in the afternoon of the same day, after she had undressed, I lifted her gently from the chair in which she had been sitting and bore her to the bed. As soon as she was composed from

the slight fatigue, I sat beside her and
embraced the opportunity to speak with
her alone. Indeed, she opened the conversation :

"I find it impossible on a sick bed to
keep up any regularity in my prayers."

"Of course," I replied, "that cannot
be helped ; but prayer does not consist in
the use of words and forms. Our sweet-
est prayers are often mere ejaculations,
sometimes not expressed at all, but only
the lifting up of a thought or desire. Besides, prayer is the constant posture of the
soul before God, in which sense we are
said to 'pray always.'"

"Yes, that is so ; and we can thus 'pray
without ceasing.' Whenever I wake in
the night, I breathe silently my prayer to
God." Then she added, after a little pause :

"I am so thankful that I was not left
to put off the great matter of my salvation
till this time of sickness and weakness.
That is a thing already done, and some-
how I have not a cloud or shadow of doubt
as to my interest in Christ."

"It is a great thing to be grateful for," I answered, "that God should put a check upon Satan, and not allow him to tempt you with any doubts or fears."

"I know," she rejoined, "that I am a sinner; but I feel that I am forgiven and accepted."

"Yes, my daughter, and we know that the blood of Christ cleanseth from all sin; and this blood has been already shed; we have only to rely on it and escape from the curse."

"I had a great struggle," she said, "when the doctor pronounced that I was bound to go like my sisters. Though I felt my hope revive a little later, yet I knew how uncertain it was, and that the least thing might set me back."

"Well, G——, we must put all that right into God's hands, and let Him dispose of you as He will—knowing that it will be ordered aright and in love."

"Yes," she replied, and repeated the lines:

"Sweet to lie passive in His hands,
And know no will but His."

Here the conversation was abruptly terminated by some one coming in. The struggle to which she referred took place at least three months before her decease. Her statement was more full to her mother than to myself. To her she mentioned that the conflict was long protracted, before she could entertain the prospect of death with composure and acquiescence. The instinct of life is strong within us all, and it was not feeble in her; and as she looked upon her husband and babe she felt that life had many and great attractions for her. Resignation, then, with her had not the faintest trace of fanaticism. Her reason and her heart appreciated the sweetness of life to one who lay in the bosom of the tenderest relations; and it was not easy, at once and forever, to resign the hope of being restored to those whom she passionately loved. Yet sharp as the conflict was, it was in keeping with her perfect unselfishness to lock it up in the secrecy of her own breast."

"The world would not have tempted

me," she said to her mother, "to reveal what was passing in my mind ; for it would have added so much to your distress to know how I was struggling against my fate."

The conflict ended in complete victory. The love of life itself was laid a sacrifice upon the altar of obedience ; and with characteristic decision it was laid there never to be taken up any more. From that moment her resignation was perfect ; and she remained in a state of restful submission to her Heavenly Father's will, till the scene was closed. Indeed, her only strong desire was that the end might not be long postponed.

"I do not want mother to be broken down by constant and painful nursing," she said ; "I wish her to be spared to you all and to my child."

It was one of the forms in which her spirit of entire self-abnegation found utterance.

February 1st, 1875.—In a conversation with her mother, she remarked:

"I do not think that I can live till Spring, for I am getting so weak. In case I should sink suddenly and be too feeble to speak, I wish you all to understand that I hope I am entirely ready to go—quite ready and willing to depart."

"I often think," her mother replied, "of the happy meeting between you and your sisters in Heaven; and do you know I am sure your influence and example had much to do in preparing them for that happy world where you will soon join them."

"Mother, do you really think so?" she inquired in a lively tone.

"Yes, I am perfectly sure of it, my daughter."

"Oh, mother, I am so glad you have told me of it."

More than these she will meet upon the mount of God, whom she has persuaded to the Saviour's feet. Several of her Sabbath-school scholars acknowledge her influence in leading them to Christ; and the last act of Christian faithfulness was her sending

for others during her illness, to entreat
them to accept the salvation now so
precious to herself. I believe they will be
given as her crown.

February 4th.—She expressed to-day
some apprehension lest her husband's
faith should be shaken by her death.

"He has such confidence in the effi-
cacy of prayer, and knows how many and
fervent have been the petitions for my recovery—when he finds it abortive, I fear
he may swing to the other extreme and
doubt the value of all prayer."

"That effect will be temporary," I
replied, "even if it should be realized at
all. He will soon recover upon the true
view that for all contingent blessings, in
reference to which God's will cannot ante-
cedently be known, our petitions must
necessarily be conditioned upon a wisdom
that is higher than our own." "Poor
fellow," she added, "I do feel so sorry
for him, "and wish he could be spared
the suffering he must undergo."

"In view of your increasing feebleness,"

I said, " had you not better make all your wishes known, and dispose of all your little effects, before you become too weak to talk or even to think much ?"

" Yes, I am doing that."

" Have you any directions to give about your babe ?"

" No; Mr. —— has promised to give her up entirely to mother; I feel no concern about her; as long as you live, you will take care of her as your own."

February 6th.—On this day her venerable grandfather, who had been with us three months, expressed great sorrow at the necessity of his departure; and offered to make this bend to our wishes if we desired him to remain. This last suggestion startled her, as implying our expectation of her immediate release.

" No," I replied; " if that were so, your grandfather would not leave. On the contrary, you may linger a good while; and his plans are so cast that he cannot well remain longer with us. We cannot tell anything about your case; you may rally and go for months, or you may take a sudden turn and go off quickly."

"Oh, I should be sorry to linger in this emaciated condition; I would only suffer with bedsores in the warm weather."

"That is not likely," was my answer; "my impression is that you will be with us but a short time now."

"That is my own view," was her response.

February 7th, Sabbath.—On this day her symptoms were increasingly bad, with swollen extremities and other troubles. I asked "if she still enjoyed peace of mind, and was conscious of a quiet, steady trust in the Redeemer."

"Yes," was the cheerful reply, "perfect peace of mind; the only thing I dread is the physical pain of dying. I cannot help remembering M——'s last struggle, and dread it for myself."

"Her case was exceptional," I answered; "it does not occur often; for in all the death-bed scenes I have witnessed, hers is the only one of the kind I ever saw.

The probabilities are that you will be spared her experience.   At any rate, leave that to God and accept all that He ordains."

"Yes," she replied, "for it will be very short, if it should occur."

Referring to her prevailing peace of mind, I inquired "whether she could distinguish between this and the listlessness arising from weakness and exhaustion?"

"I am sometimes too weak even to think; but at other moments I am stronger, especially during the hours of night; and then my peace is greatest, as I pour out my heart before God.   But pray constantly for me," she added.

I could only reply:

"There is not an hour of the day that I do not pray for you, my darling."

February 9th, Tuesday.—Her weakness prevented her from speaking, except to indicate her wants.   It also provoked the dreadful cough which racked her frame, so that conversation was almost precluded, though so much desired on both sides. But wishing to know her spiritual state as the case went on, I again inquired : "G——, are you still in the sweet and trustful frame of which you have before spoken, having no dread of the change that is awaiting you ?"

"Yes," she replied, "strangely so ; I have always recoiled from the thought of dying ; and when I saw my sisters so calm, I wondered how it was possible and thought I could not be like them in their situation. But I feel entire willingness to go—only," she added, "it will be so dreadful-dreary to you all when I am gone, though I say it."

"Ah ! you must not think of us, my child ; God knows the house will be dark and chill enough, when you are gone ; but the great concern with you is to be ready for that stupendous change."

"Indeed it is," she replied ; "death is solemn enough when it meets you in the streets, or read about it as happening to others ; but it is another thing when it sits down before you on the bed, and you must look at it face to face, day after day, for yourself."

"What a blessed grace is given you, then, my child, if you can do so; and with all that it imports, feel that for you the sting of death is taken away."

"Yes," she rejoined, "and it is all of grace."

February 11th, Thursday. — Another snatch of conversation:

"One thing is strange to me," she said, "I have not been able to read my Bible much of late, yet its passages come up to me with so much freshness and power— frequently when I wake out of sleep, at night, this is the case."

"There is nothing strange in it," I answered, "since one of the ways in which the Holy Spirit performs His office as Comforter, is by bringing to our remembrance whatsoever Christ has said."

"Yes," she rejoined, "and that is exactly what the Saviour promised to His disciples."

After a pause she added:

"One thing has greatly comforted me: I thought that when I should be dying, the uppermost feeling would be the anticipation of meeting my sisters in Heaven. But that is quite in the background; the great joy is the thought of being with my Saviour."

After this she only said:

"There is so much I would like to say to you all; but I cannot talk, because of this great weakness and this awful cough, which begins as soon as I open my lips."

"And that prevents us from saying much to you, my child; for you cannot help answering back, and so we are all shut up together."

February 12th, Friday.—After breakfast her linen was changed, and her bed prepared, as she reclined for a few moments upon the lounge. Happening to enter the room just then, I exclaimed:

"How comfortable you look! It must be a relief to change your position."

"Oh, no," was the response, "I must get back as soon as I can."

She was replaced in bed in the sitting posture she had preferred for the week

past, propped up with pillows. I did not
apprehend the case ; for seeing her, as I
supposed, comfortable as usual, I left the
house to execute an arrangement previously made with her—that I should go
to the cemetery and look at the tomb in
which she was soon to be placed, the care
of which we had been compelled for some
time to neglect. Thence I proceeded to
the postoffice for letters, so as to avoid any
further absence during the day. Upon
entering the house, I was startled by a
sudden call over the banisters to hurry up-
stairs. She had missed me and called for
me. When I entered the room, a glance
revealed that her feet were already in the
cold river.

"Speak to her," said the mother, "and
see if she will recognise you."

"Not for the world," I answered.

She was in a gentle sleep, with her head
resting one side on her pillow. A half-
hour's watching and then the sleep deepened into that which knows no waking.
At half-past 11 o'clock A. M., without the

quivering of a muscle or the heaving of a sigh, her patient spirit had joined the worshipers on high. Our last prayer was heard; and the last dread that threw a shade over her dying hour, was spared to us and to her.

February 14, 1875, Sabbath.—On the afternoon of a beautiful Sabbath the largest cortege I have ever seen at a private funeral, followed her remains to their last resting place; and a whole community mourned for one whom so many loved, as we put her to sleep by the side of the sisters whom she had followed to the skies.

Sitting down in the twilight in our dismantled home, we thought of the " Mansion " above, already furnished with the household waiting to greet us on the threshold when we, too, shall be called.

" These border-lands are calm and still,
    And solemn are their silent shades ;
And my heart welcomes them, until
    The light of life's long evening fades.

" I heard them spoken of with dread,
    As fearful and unquiet places ;
Shades, where the living and the dead
    Look sadly in each other's faces.

" But since Thy hand hath led me here,
    And I have seen the border-land ;
Seen the dark river flowing near,
    Stood on its brink, as now I stand—

" There has been nothing to alarm
    My trembling soul ; how could I fear
While thus encircled with Thine arm ?
    I never felt Thee half so near.

" They say the waves are dark and deep,
    That faith has perished in the river ;
They speak of death with fear, and weep
    Shall my soul perish ? Never ! never !

" And since I first was brought so near
    The stream that flows to the Dead Sea,
I think that it grows more clear
    And shallow than it used to be.

" I cannot see the golden gate
    Unfolding yet to welcome me ;
I cannot yet anticipate
    The joy of Heaven's jubilee—

" But I will calmly watch and pray,
    Until I hear my Saviour's voice
Calling my happy soul away,
    To see His glory and rejoice."

VI.

" But there is more than I can see,
And what I see, I leave unsaid,
Nor speak it, knowing Death has made
His darkness beautiful with thee."

"Your mother is ill—come to her at once." Such was the rasping message delivered one crisp November morning, forty years ago. Ah! we have but one mother on earth ; who can replace her in our thought? She who bore us in the walls of her flesh, in the strange community of a dual life : she who nourished us, in feeble infancy, from her own substance : she whose smile woke us to the first response of love : she whose constant sympathy assuaged the sorrows of childhood, and whose guardian providence shielded from the snares of opening manhood : she to whom was paid the homage of youthful hearts, mounting to such lower worship as may be given to a mortal : such was the mother who, in nature's extremity, craved the presence of her son.

Through the life of a generation she had filled the responsible position of a Christian pastor's wife, for which she was eminently fitted both by nature and by grace. Possessing a vigorous intellect, enlarged by generous culture, she found opportunity even amidst domestic cares for its continual improvement. The habit of early rising gave her an hour before the day began its busy hum ; and through the long working hours she would snatch brief intervals for reading. Some solid book was always on her table, and some subject always on her mind for study and conversation. Thus she became the companion of her husband, sharing his thoughts and pursuits ; and the transient clergyman who passed a night beneath her roof, never failed to carry away a deep impression of her intelligence and worth.

For the office of a mother she was sin-

gularly qualified.   Always the teacher of
her young children, she had the rare
faculty of letting herself down into their
minds, and of feeling a real sympathy with
all their emotions.   So entire was the ascendancy she thereby acquired, that her
sons, in all the rudeness of boyhood, never
knew the time when they would not cheer-
fully exchange the sports and playmates
of the field for the quiet conversation of
their mother at her work-table.   Mingling
gentleness with decision, she was able to
add guidance to discipline.   Seizing those
moments when they yielded themselves
without prejudice to her influence, her
speech distilled upon them as dew upon
the mown grass.   She never sermonized ;
but dropping occasional remarks with little
apparent design, furnished them with
maxims suited to all conditions in life.
Let not the reader regard these as mere
common-places uttered to fill a period.
Who that looks back upon the critical passages of his life, will not bless God for the
gift of a pious mother—feeling that her

hand has plucked him from ruin.   There
are seasons of recklessness in youth when
we can place our profane feet upon everything save a mother's love ; and a mother's
love has often quenched the fire which
authority and force would have fanned into
a consuming flame.   This pious mother
met with a pious mother's reward.   Of
her eight children, four preceded her to
the world of bliss ; four wept around her
grave ; but these four trust in their mother's
God, and the two sons preach that Jesus
in whom they believe, and whom their
mother confessed on her dying bed.

This much is written, not as the record
of a long and holy life, but as preparing
for the sketch of an unusual experience in
her last moments.   After years spent in
close communion with God we would
naturally expect an end of peace, if not of
joy; but rarely on earth is a departing
saint permitted to leave such a testimony,
lighting up the Valley of the Shadow of
Death with such a shining from the "upper
day."

In the commencement of her sickness her hope was for one day greatly obscured ; and she called to her husband and children to pray that Christ would reveal Himself to her faith, and that she might enjoy the fullest assurance of her acceptance with God. As may be anticipated, she came out of the cloud, saying :

"I feel that your prayers have been heard ; I am delivered from darkness and see and feel Jesus to be my Saviour."

From this moment she rejoiced in an unclouded assurance of hope to the end. As she lay often apparently asleep, her frequent exclamations, "Wonderful love !" "Precious salvation !" evinced that her soul was absorbed in adoring views of God's love and mercy in Christ. More than once, speaking of Christ as a complete Saviour, she exclaimed :

"What a wretched religion the Unitarian has—he has no God for his Saviour."

On one occasion a portion of the Eighty-ninth Psalm was read to her ; she responded with animation to the verses which set forth the perpetuity of God's covenant with His people, and to the person who prayed she remarked:

"I love to hear you pray, because you dwell so much upon God's covenant—that is my hope."

To this she several times referred, rejoicing that God's love was spontaneous, and that His favor was not doled out according to the measure of our poor services. When asked if death was at all terrible, she replied:

"Not so now, but it may be otherwise at the last; pray for special grace in that trying moment."

On the Sabbath preceding her death, she said to one of her sons who had preached:

"I wish I could have heard you to-day; you preached on the believer's future likeness to Christ in Heaven."

He replied: "Mother, you will soon know that mystery fully."

"Oh, it is a sweet promise," was her immediate response.

In the evening of this Sabbath, the family alone being with her, she asked for a hymn to be sung; the words, "Come, Holy Spirit, Heavenly Dove," were chosen; it must have been a foretaste of Heaven to her, for at the end of each line she would exclaim, lifting her hands:

"Oh, how sweet!"

The last sad day came at length, and gloom settled upon every face. She was told, "You are very low, very near to death;" her calm reply betrayed no surprise:

"I suppose the doctor has done his best; I shall soon be at rest; how sweet it will be!"

A few directions were given to her daughters, and she assumed the posture of one waiting to depart. As the day rolled on, she seemed impatient to be gone: "Come, Lord Jesus," "Why delayeth His chariot?" and such like expressions, indicated how her spirit panted after rest. She was asked:

"Why are you anxious to die?"

" It is better to be in Heaven."

" Why do you wish to be in Heaven ?"

" Because it is a place of holiness ; that is the chief attraction."

As the night was closing in, she said :

" I thought all day the time was about fixed for me to go."

Being asked what she thought then, her reply was :

" God acts like a Sovereign in His own way."

She was reminded that there is an appointed time for man upon the earth.

" Yes," was the answer, "and that bound none shall pass."

Being asked if she felt that all was well with her, she replied :

" Yes, I am very sure."

From this moment she sank into what appeared to us a state of delirium, failing to recognise any one around her or to respond intelligently to anything said to her. During the hours she remained in this condition, many painful efforts were made to recall her to us—her husband especially took her hand in his and sought a recognition, but in vain. Various questions were put, which showed that all intercourse with this world was barred; she knew neither face nor voice of those she loved most on earth. Appeal after appeal was made to memory and to every other faculty, for one sign of remembrance; until these fruitless attempts were abandoned, and a gloomy silence settled upon all within that chamber of death. Then followed a scene such as the writer has never witnessed before or since; which so completely changed his views concerning the gloom of the believer's death, that the recital may perhaps be profitable to others. Happening to be lying across the bed with his head very near to hers, without any motive of which he was conscious moving him to the act, he whispered softly in her ear the words of Paul, "There is, therefore, now no condemnation to them which are in Christ Jesus;" when, to the amazement of all present, she took the passage out of his mouth, adding the remaining words—"who walk not after the flesh, but after the Spirit." It would be impossible for any description to convey the impression produced by this incident; one must have been able to contrast it with the vain efforts made through successive hours to win one token of earthly recognition, to know what it imported to this sad company. The husband was seated upon a trunk in the corner of the room; when suddenly approaching the bed, he exclaimed: "This is wonderful—try her with another verse." These words were whispered in her ear in the softest possible tone, "God is our refuge and strength;" when again she took up the inspired words and finished them—"a very present help in trouble." Again it was whispered to her, "I have loved thee with an everlasting love;" to which she instantly rejoined, "and with loving-kindness have I drawn thee." Desiring of testing how far she was alive to spiritual things, while dead to those of earth, that involved and complex passage in Job was cited—"I know that my Re-

deemer liveth ;" when to the wonder of all
present the whole context was, after a moment's pause, correctly repeated : " And
that he shall stand at the latter day upon
the earth ; and though after my skin worms
destroy this body, yet in my flesh shall I
see God ; whom I shall see for myself, and
mine eyes shall behold, and not another."
Penetrated with awe and weeping for joy,
only one more utterance was solicited as
the expression of her personal faith and
hope : the words of Paul were begun—" I
know whom I have believed ;" her dying
lips concluded the testimony of an assured
believer, by instantly adding—"and am
persuaded that he is able to keep that
which I have committed unto him against
that day."

Here, then, is a soul in such a state as
to be utterly inaccessible to impressions
from the material world, while perfectly
open to those from the spiritual. Neither
the tenderest domestic ties, nor the asso
ciations of a long life, have power to recall
her to earth ; whilst the sacred language

of the Scriptures rivets her attention, and
commands the homage both of mind and
heart.   There is but one solution of the
case possible ; and with the admission of
this, the entire mystery disappears.   In
this dying hour the Holy Ghost was finishing the work of grace, completing the likeness of the saint to her blessed Head, and
fitting her for immediate entrance into the
world of glory.   She was, therefore, absorbed in spiritual themes; and the language of the Bible was recognised, because
it coincided with the current of thought
and feeling which was then indulged.
What seemed to those around her couch
to be delirium, was simply seclusion from
the world in which they moved ; so that
nothing which human affection could suggest, gained the attention for a moment.

Does not this explanation of the case go
far to unravel the mysterious incidents of
many a dying experience ? Those seraphic
smiles playing over the face, like the sheet-
lightning which sports upon a summer
cloud—those typical gestures pointing as

to some real presence, which the eye is
unable to discern—the joyful recognition
of beautiful spirits, who seem to beckon
the departing soul towards the glory that
is beyond : all these things so often recur-
ring, and throwing such awe upon sur-
viving friends as pregnant hints of the
Eternity at other times so far away—may
they not be only the natural expressions
of spiritual desires and affections, wrought
in the heart by the Holy Spirit in the hour
when His work is finished on the human
soul ?   May they not be simply the reflection of the grace that is wrought within
the believer, when he is " made meet to
be partaker of the inheritance of the saints
in light ? " And may it not be lawful to
conclude that these cases, which seem to
us so rare, are but types of all the rest ?
And that while God will not suffer the
secrets of the eternal world to be betrayed
by any, He allows these hints to be given
of the luxury in dying in every case where
the likeness to Christ is completed, and
the last look of faith is taken of Him

whom the soul loveth?

This, then, was the lesson coming out
of a great filial sorrow, the blessedness of
death to the people of God. Says the
Apostle, "The sting of death is sin;"
but if the guilt of sin is cancelled, and its
pollution cleansed, and its being destroyed,
and its very presence removed, what then
becomes of the sting? There surely is a
last act of faith before it is swallowed up
in sight—a last tear of penitence, in which
the stain is washed away—a last touch of
the Spirit, in which indwelling sin is forever removed and the transfiguration into
the Redeemer's image is rendered complete. Can imagination conceive, or language describe, the joy of such an experience? The process may be shut up
within an instant, just as the spirit is being
released from its battered tenement of clay;
or it may be drawn through hours of deepening sanctification, in which the believer
shall be closeted alone with the blessed
Comforter. In either case, the believer
shall spring from earth to Heaven with the

shout of perfect joy, in the possession of a
perfected holiness. Whatever the pangs
of dissolution may appear to be, they are
only the storm which ruffles the surface of
the sea, but cannot disturb the calm of the
unfathomed depths beneath.

There is no more fitting close of this
sketch than Pope's free translation of
Hadrian's celebrated Latin hymn:

"Vital spark of heavenly flame,
  Quit, O quit this mortal frame;
  Trembling, hoping, lingering, flying,
  O the pain, the bliss of dying!
  Cease, fond nature, cease thy strife,
  And let me languish into life.

"Hark! they whisper, angels say,
  'Sister spirit, come away.'
  What is this absorbs me quite,
  Steals my senses, shuts my sight;
  Drowns my spirit, draws my breath?
  Tell me, my soul, can this be death?

"The world recedes, it disappears;
  Heaven opens on my eyes—my ears
  With sounds seraphic ring;
  Lend, lend your wings, I mount, I fly;
  O Grave, where is thy victory?
  O Death, where is thy sting?"

VII.

"Gone home! Gone home! The door through which
   she vanished
    Closed with a jar, and left us here alone.
We stand without in tears, forlorn and banished,
    Longing to follow where one loved has gone."

Five times "the waters of a full cup
had been wrung out" to these stricken
parents; and five times they had said, each
to the other: "God is merciful—you at
least are spared." The supreme sorrow
had not yet been felt, until it should be
written: "He sitteth alone and keepeth
silence, because he hath borne it upon him."

Through a ministry of many years it had
been his office to comfort the bereaved,
and to say, "a Father of the fatherless,
and a Judge of the widows, is God in His
holy habitation." Yet the shadow of one
grief sent ever the chill to his heart, with
the wonder how it could be endured. It
was the sharp blade cleaving through the

"dual unity" of marriage, with but the one-half left to live and mourn. As quaintly but impressively described in a private letter, "there is no stroke so disorganizing —it is breaking the hub of the wheel and leaving the surrounding circle disabled and dislocated." This was the lesson to be learned in the final sorrow, *how one could be slain and live.*

The Scriptures speak with unutterable tenderness of "the wife of thy youth," and of "the wife of thy covenant;" yet romantic as may be the love which greets the bride, it is not the holy thing into which it grows through the consecration of the after years. The bloom of youth may have faded forever; instead of which may be the frost of age and the furrows of care. But how these speak of a long ministry of love—of common joys and sorrows, with which a "stranger intermeddleth not"—of mutual burdens borne, and mutual counsels given—of that hidden fellowship in which both took retreat from the burning trials and fretting discords of earth! In the light of such memories, how beautifully transfigured becomes the time-scarred brow, and the face with its seams of faithful and loving service! Though the arms may tremble in the patriarchal embrace in which the fervor of earthly passion has cooled, there remains the grateful remembrance of life-long sympathy, of mutual dependence and care.

"The heart knoweth his own bitterness" when the web of these associations is rudely torn by the hand of Death. This is the bereavement now to be recorded. It came with appalling suddenness at the last. A severe illness continuing through a summer and necessitating travel, had yielded to medical treatment; and a year's delightful convalescence gave promise of ultimate recovery. Alas, that disease should thus slumber in the frame, with the seeds of death planted in its members! The suspended blow came with crushing effect, after this brief reprieve. At first it was regarded as the recurrence of the old disorder—shifting its disguise as it was baffled

by the physician's skill; until, after a
night's discomposure, the heart ceased to
beat, and she was gone! Without a suspicion of immediate danger, she had time
only to say, "I believe I am dying," and
within a moment came that far-off look
which fills the beholder with awe, as it
gazes beyond things present into the deep
unseen.   Not a word of farewell could be
spoken; as

> "Closer, closer her steps
> Come to the dark abysm ;
> Closer, death to her lips
> Presses the awful chrism."

The curtain had fallen suddenly between
the two worlds—she in that, and we in
this.   Oh, how the heart has ached to
speak that unspoken word to her—and to
hear it spoken back across that mysterious
border!   But the law of Faith cannot be
broken for a momentary indulgence:
"Blessed are they that have not seen, and
yet have believed."   Alas, there are many

> "Who to the verge have followed those they love,
> And on the insuperable threshold stand,
> With cherished names its speechless calm reprove,
> And stretch in the abyss their ungrasped hand."

Death has the strange power of sanctifying all whom he may touch ; they become to us as the angels of God. The memory of them crystallizes into a living form unsubstantial and pure as the light, which glides into the soul and abides a sweet and solemn presence there. Yet partial as the hand may be which draws this portrait, it shall be a faithful likeness still.

The attention of a stranger would be arrested by the air of repose diffused over her person. It was characteristic of her girlhood, so far removed from the giddiness of the young coquette. It was not the sedateness of the matron, into which it may have later grown ; still less was it the sluggishness of a stagnant mind. Few enjoyed more than she the humorous side of life, or whose sensibilities responded more quickly to all that was gracious and tender. It was not inertness, nor could it be termed even sobriety ; for there was a glow in her manner which won to her side the young as well as the old. The word ''repose'' alone describes it—and it made her so

restful to others.   Whatever cares might
oppress, or passions disturb, to come into
her presence was to come into the region
of calm.   It was like a breeze from the sea
which took the fever from the brow.   And
so we learned to lean upon her, whose
magic touch could soothe our ruffled tem-
pers into quietness like her own.   This
above all others is the home-attribute,
which makes it the haven of rest to the
weary.   It is this peacefulness throwing
its grateful shade between us and the
scorching sun, that makes   .

> " Domestic happiness the only bliss
>   Of Paradise that has survived the fall."

Hers was the repose of a deep, calm nature that lay beneath, suggestive not of
weakness but of strength.   It was the repose of the sea, with the wind rippling and
the sunbeam dancing upon it, as it rested
upon the quiet depths below.   Hers was
the calmness of a self-contained nature—
not indifferent to anything around it, nor
shallow enough to be agitated thereby;
but drawing up from unseen depths a

strength to be calm amidst earthly storms. A masterly will held her at anchor amidst the drifting tides. Her convictions of truth and duty were unalterable, for they were rooted in the foundations of her own being. This resulted from the independence which would take no opinions upon trust, but cast them into the mould of her own thought—and for which she was always prepared to render a reason. Her opinions ripened thus into convictions, and these into principles which became to her the rule of conduct. But in this there was no offensive self-assertion. Her independence never degenerated into dogmatism, nor her will into wilfulness. Her convictions were for herself, to be the guide of her own actions.

In the calm of a nature thus self-poised there lay a quiet force, which went forth with a silent yet magnetic control of all with whom she came in contact. Its pressure was like that of the atmosphere, so equal on every side as scarcely to be recognised. Like the forces in the material

world, it was the more irrestible from the
silence with which it moved.   It overcame
before its presence was suspected, and its
gentleness disarmed opposition.   There
was no circle in which this quiet supremacy
was not gained.   In her household it was
an influence pervading every department
of service, with a sort of omnipresence
which dispensed with the necessity of personal inspection anywhere.   It was an
ascendancy from force of character, so
restful in its quietness that all leaned upon
it in the hour of trial.   It was the queenly
trait in her career, that rose with the
emergencies which called it forth.   In the
deep sorrows through which she passed,
her calm submission was an angel's strength
to all around her; whilst in each, she
mounted to a higher trust in Him who
was preparing her for the eternal rest.

The virtues, as well as the vices, grow
together in the cluster.   It will occasion
no surprise that transparent honesty
marked the character just depicted.   Her
truthfulness was so punctilious, that it

stumbled even over the social courtesies
in which the slightest prevarication was
implied. And the strategy was sometimes
amusing, which substituted a judicious
silence for the conventionalisms in which
the charge of falsehood can be evaded only
by construing them as unmeaning. This
sincerity was, however, accompanied with
such grace of manner as never to seem
harsh or brusque ; whilst it had the advantage of securing that measure of confidence
which is accorded only to perfect honesty
of mind and heart. She was thus the
truest of the true ; and so carried her heart
in her hand, that her speech was ever the
echo of her thought.

She possessed in unusual degree the
womanly instinct of penetrating the character of those with whom she was suddenly
brought in contact. In using this term,
instinct, no metaphysical analysis is designed. If it be a process of reasoning,
its method is too subtle and rapid to be
easily traced ; and it seems to move with
the certainty of an instinct. But whether

reason or instinct, it is a kindly gift of
Providence for woman's protection amid
the snares of life.   Unless a false glare has
captured her fancy, this penetrating insight
into others seldom deceives ; and after the
great peril of marriage is passed, and the
instinct is evoked for the benefit of her
household, it becomes the faithful sentinel
whose timely warning it is safe to heed.
This gift of, not second, but first sight
must of course be supplemented by a sound
judgment,   in   order to form a judicious
counsellor ; and when to both is added the
discretion which tells when to be silent
and when to speak, all the elements are
combined which made the subject of this
sketch the most trustworthy of friends.
Her perceptions were so clear that her
judgment of men had seldom to be revised ;
and her prudence was so consummate, that
in no instance was the confidence reposed
in her ever betrayed.

The modesty of nature prompts us to
throw a veil of reserve over the feelings
which · are sacred.   It is not easy, for

example, to speak to others of the domestic affections; and it must be a fit occasion that justifies the revelation. Hence the difficulty of tracing another's religious history, which must, to a large extent, remain a secret between the soul and God. Certainly with those constitutionally reserved, the inner life can only be discovered as it is revealed in the outward character and walk. It is thus we are forced to estimate the piety of her to whom this tribute of love is paid. Her spiritual exercises must be interpreted to us through

"Those thousand decencies that daily flowed
From all her words and actions."

Her habit was to spend the early morning hour in devotion, before others of the household were awake—a habit dating back to the period of her marriage at an early age. Thus she entered upon the duties of the day fresh from communion with God, and her face shining like that of Moses when he came down from the Mount.

The successive bereavements through

which she passed, already detailed, purified
her spirit and lent new attractions to the
eternal home in which her children were
gathered.   The sadness of her heart was
not allowed, however, to throw its gloom
over the house in which a younger generation of grandchildren were growing up
around her.   Life must, at least, be kept
free from bitterness for them, who should
in their time have sorrows of their own.
Yet it was easy to see that in lonely and
pensive hours her communings were with
another world, and that she was ripening
for her own translation.   A gracious intimation of this was afforded in the severe
illness previously mentioned, better understood by her than by us who were so un-
willing to look to the end ; and in the year's
subsequent reprieve her watchfulness was
not for an instant remitted.   Expressions
dropped daily from her lips, the significance of which we failed to recognise ; and
a hundred little actions have since been
recalled, which showed her departure
always before her mind.   Though the

summons came suddenly at the last, our surprise was not hers. With her lamp trimmed, and waiting for the coming of her Lord, she was ready to enter in and sit at the Marriage Feast.

"To her it was not more than the sudden lifting of a
    latch,
Nought but a step into the open air out of a tent
Already luminous with light that shines through
    its transparent folds."

The following extract from a memorial paper adopted by an Association of Christian Ladies over which she presided, will show how she was embalmed in their affections:

"Nearly twenty years ago quite a number of us organized ourselves together for the purpose of benevolent and Christian labors; and she by whose vacant seat we now stand to-day with such sorrowful hearts, was chosen from among us to be our guide, our counsellor and our leader—and we called her President.

"Many of us were just entering upon life's morning, the future all glorious before us, with the rainbow of hope undimmed by sorrow's touch. Others were already bearing the heat and burden of the day, and were oft-times weary with the load of care. And, again, there were those whose eyes were turned to the brighter and more perfect day, but whose feet were oft-times tottering and very feeble. But to one and all, of every age, our President was a day-spring of joy—ever rejoicing with those that did rejoice, and weeping with those that wept. In sorrow and in trial she ever strengthened by her counsel, and cheered by her sympathy, herself bearing a part of our burden. As a Society, we sometimes halted by the way ; or like a streamlet with rippled, ruffled surface, made murmur as we moved ; until with one common impulse we would throw all the trouble over on the broad, calm, deep nature—whose serious depth we then, alas ! but partially understood ; but now has come the full knowledge of its power and of our great loss. We know her as she was—strong, yet gentle ; firm, but tender ; a true Chris-

tian, with every womanly virtue. * * *
In her beautiful womanhood, during all
these years she went in and out among us,
always looked for, always welcomed, ever
at her post, until the dawning of that day
when it was said, 'she sleeps;' and from
that sleep we may not awaken her. But
there is a forward looking, and an upward;
and may we not pray that her mantle cover
us; and that with united and renewed
strength we follow on where she would
have led—even as she would now say to
us, 'Come up higher.'"

"'Tis only when they spring to heaven that angels
 Reveal themselves to you; they sit all day
 Beside you, and lie down at night by you,
 Who care not for their presence—muse or sleep—
 And all at once they leave you and you know them."

But what a sarcasm it is upon the wisdom of man, that his treasures should be
known only through their loss! The
separation came after the sweet possession
of seven and forty years, and left us bankrupt. It was a sorrow wholly by itself.

What is to be done with a love which
belongs only to one, when that one is
gone and cannot take it up? It cannot
perish, for it has become part of our own
being.   What shall we do with a lost love,
which wanders like a ghost through all the
chambers of the soul, only to feel how
empty they are?   There may be those
about us who are very dear; but this love
cannot be divided among them, for it is
incapable of distribution.   What remains
but to send it upward, until it finds her to
whom it belongs by right of concentration
for more than forty years.   In the unselfishness of love we wish her joy in her
immortal ascension, willing ourselves to
take the loss that hers may be the everlasting gain.

The richest grace, does it not lie in the
heaviest sorrow?   Was it not in "the
burning fiery furnace" the three Hebrew
children saw "the form of the fourth, like
the Son of God," walking in the midst of
the fire?   It was when "Moses drew near
to the thick darkness where God was,"

that he spake with Him face to face and heard His voice. And how often it is in "the thick darkness" Jehovah reveals Himself as the Comforter of His people! The cloud which settles down upon a desolate home, He graciously fills with His own presence: we find it to be "secret of His Tabernacle," the "pavilion" in which He "will show His Covenant." The Divine love breaks through the gloom, as once it burst through the terrors of Sinai and the darkness of Calvary. It is not what we would have chosen; but in this dark cloud we learn that it is best sometimes to be alone with Him. The earthly lights are put out, that no earthly love may come in between Him and us. It is the miracle of love— this stringing of the harp to a greater tension, that the praise may hereafter rise to higher and sweeter notes before the Throne, when we shall carry the memories of earth to Heaven and pour them into song forever. May it be the finishing lesson of the one great sorrow near the end of life—how through the few remaining

days to be "quiet as a child that is weaned
of his mother;" and to know the sufficiency
of the Divine fulness, before it becomes
the joy and the portion of Heaven!

MIZPAH—Genesis xxxi. 49.

"We never used the word, while thou and I
　　Walked close together in life's working way;
There was no need for it, when hand and eye
　　Might meet content and faithful every day.

"But now with anguish from a stricken heart,
　　Mizpah I cry; the Lord keep watch between
Thy life and mine, that death has riven apart;
　　Thy life beyond the awful veil unseen,
And my poor broken being, which must glide
　　Through ways familiar to us both, till death
Shall of a surety lead me to thy side,
　　Beyond the chance and change of mortal breath.
Mizpah! Yea, Lord, in all my bitter pain
I trust God keepeth watch betwixt us twain.

"Thy lips are dumb from which I used to hear
　　Strong words of counsel, tender words of praise;
But I must go my way, without the cheer
　　And sunshine of thy presence, all my days.
But God keep watch my ways and days upon,
　　On all I do, on all I bear, for thee;
My work is left me, though my mate is gone;
　　A solemn trust has been bequeathed to me.
I take the task thy languid hand laid down
　　That wintry morning, for mine own alway;
And may the Giver of both Cross and Crown
　　Pronounce me faithful on our meeting day.
Mizpah! the word gives comfort to my pain;
I know God keepeth watch betwixt us twain."

The following lines are here appended; which first appeared anonymously, many years ago, in Blackwood's Magazine. They are singularly appropriate at the close of all these sketches:

"The veil has dropped. Her spirit now
  Intense with life, hath soared above;
  And dwelleth where the seraphs bow,
  And sing their holy hymns of love.
The seed hath sprung into a tree;
The flower hath burst its bud, the immortal soul is
  free.

"Oh, death is full of life. Naught dies
  But that which should. Earth takes its own,
  That the eternal may arise
  And dwell by the eternal throne.
Death is the full outshining light
Of that unending morn, which knows no night.

"Death can but take his own. The earth
  Can only ask what she did give;
  Then let the Heaven-born mind have birth,
  That it eternally may live.
Oh, let it cast its outer frame,
And rise a living soul to Him from whom it came.

"Gaze on that form.   Nay, lift thine eye
    And gaze above.   She is not here ;
    She hath arisen to worlds on high,
    And dwelleth in a purer sphere.
This frame of dust she hath laid down,
To gain a robe of light and a celestial crown.

"The veil has dropped.   Her inward eye
    Has seen the mysteries of God ;
    And onward through the star-paved sky
    Mid Heaven's bright glory she has trod :
Angels are guiding her along,
While her sweet voice unites in their triumphal song."

CONCLUSION.

Nothing is needed to complete the pre-ceding story but this additional note.

Of the eight who once gathered within this now broken home, two alone remain under the shadow of a common grief. One elder sister is spared, who watched beside the couch and closed the eyes of the other four that have gone up to. sit in the "golden chairs"—spared to a sweet ministry of love during a mother's failing years—still longer spared to assuage a father's loneliness and grief.

The house is not cheerless even in its sor-row. The voices of a younger generation resound within its chambers—so full of hope that they make a future even for the old. Better than all, the light of that love which says, " I have chosen thee in the furnace of affliction," breaks through the gloom ; and, like a star, guides those who weep to Him upon the Throne who shall wipe away the tears.

"Blessed be God, even the Father of our Lord Jesus Christ, the Father of mercies, and the God of all comfort; who comforteth us in all our tribulation, that we may be able to comfort them which are in any trouble, by the comfort wherewith we ourselves are comforted of God."

"After this I beheld, and lo, a great multitude, which no man could number, of all nations, and kindreds, and people, and tongues, stood before the Throne, and before the Lamb, clothed with white robes, and palms in their hands. * * * And one of the Elders answered, saying unto me, What are these which are arrayed in white robes? and whence came they? And I said unto him, Sir, thou knowest. And he said to me, These are they which came out of great tribulation, and have washed their robes, and made them white in the blood of the Lamb. Therefore are they before the throne of God, and serve Him day and night in His temple : and He that

sitteth on the Throne shall feed them.
They shall hunger no more, neither thirst
any more; neither shall the sun light on
them, nor any heat. For the Lamb which
is in the midst of the Throne shall feed
them, and shall lead them unto living
fountains of waters; and God shall wipe
away all tears from their eyes."

> " O, city of the jasper wall,
>   And of the pearly gate!
> For thee, amid the storms of life,
>   Our weary spirits wait.
> We long to walk the streets of gold
>   No mortal feet have trod;
> We long to worship at the shrine,
>   The temple of our God!
> O home of bliss! O land of light!
> Where falleth neither shade nor blight—
> Of every land the brightest, best—
> When shall we there find peace and rest?

> " O city where they need no light
>   Of sun, or moon or star,
> Could we with eye of faith but see
>   How bright thy mansions are,
> How soon our doubts would fly away!
>   How strong our trust would grow,
> Until our hearts should lean no more
>   On trifles here below!
> O home of bliss! O land of light!
> Where falleth neither shade nor blight—
> Of every land the brightest, best—
> When shall we there find peace and rest?

"O city where the shining gates
  Shut out all grief and sin,
Well may we yearn amidst earth's strife
  Thy holy peace to win !
Yet must we meekly bear the cross,
  Nor seek to lay it down
Until our Father brings us home
  And gives the promised crown.
O home of bliss !   O land of light !
Where falleth neither shade nor blight—
Of every land the brightest, best —
Soon shall we there find peace and rest."

www.ingramcontent.com/pod-product-compliance
Lightning Source LLC
Chambersburg PA
CBHW020547270326
41927CB00006B/746